You Are Not Your ADHD

The Women's Guide To
Hacking Your ADHD Brain
So You Can Work With It
Rather Than Fight Against It

Lou O'Connell MBE

ii

You Are Not Your ADHD
The Women's Guide to Hacking Your ADHD Brain So
You Can Work With It Rather Than Fight Against It
Copyright© Lou O'Connell MBE, 2024

ISBN: 9781068768408 Paperback

Published by: Inspired By Publishing

The strategies outlined in this book are provided primarily for educational purposes. Every effort has been made to trace the copyright holders and obtain their permission for the use of copyright material.

The information and resources provided in this book are based on the author's personal experiences. As such, any outcomes or results described are specific to the author and may not be indicative of your own experience. There is no guarantee that you will achieve similar results after reading this book.

This book is not intended to replace professional medical care or advice. Always seek the advice of a doctor or qualified mental health professional if you have any concerns about your mental or physical health.

The author reserves the right to make changes to the content and assumes no responsibility or liability for any actions taken by purchasers or readers of this material.

Dedication

To all of the incredible women who have navigated life with the untamed brilliance of an ADHD mind, this book is for you. For every moment you felt out of place, for every time you doubted yourself and for every triumph you earned that went unrecognised. This book is dedicated to your courage, your spirit and the extraordinary light you bring to the world.

Acknowledgements

I would like to start by saying thank you to Chloë and the team at Inspired by Publishing for helping me turn my dream of being a published author into a reality. Without their help, I have no doubts that my wonderful ADHD brain would still be procrastinating.

To the Biglies, my soul sisters: Thank you for your unwavering friendship, laughter and understanding. Your constant support has been a source of strength and inspiration.

To the Squirrels, my ADHD coaches tribe: Your guidance and wisdom have been invaluable. Thank you for helping me navigate the complexities of ADHD with grace and resilience.

To all of the clients I've worked with over nearly three decades in both paid and voluntary roles, and to those I continue to work with: Working with each of you has been a rewarding and enlightening experience. Your stories, challenges and triumphs have significantly influenced this book and my understanding of mental health, wellbeing, bereavement and more recently, ADHD. Thank you for trusting me with your journeys.

To my cousin Lorraine, who, despite the physical distance between us, knows me better than anyone else in the world. I love our regular video chats, your steadfast support means the world to me.

To my Dad: Thank you for always believing in me. Your faith in my abilities has been a guiding light throughout my life.

To my Mum: Though you were taken from us too soon, your courage and the way you lived your life continues to inspire me every day. Your legacy of bravery and strength lives on in everything I do.

I am deeply grateful to each of you for your love, support and belief in me. This book is as much yours as it is mine.

Contents

Contents

Introduction
Unseen Struggles,
the Masked Woman

"I've accidentally spent my whole life making sure everyone around me was comfortable, only to realise I never felt comfortable the whole time."

– Unknown

In today's world, women with ADHD often find themselves lacking the support they deserve. It's not easy to admit, but it's an unfortunate reality. If you're reading this book, chances are you've experienced firsthand the shortcomings of the current health system. Perhaps you're feeling uncertain, or overwhelmed. Maybe you've even worried about early signs of dementia, as I once did. Or perhaps you've spent years feeling like a shit adult because you've struggled to do the things that others around you seem to do easily…

No more! I see you and you are no longer alone in this struggle! You've come to the right place and as you'll find out, there's lots of us out there.

This book will help you understand your ADHD brain and allow you to see that, up until now, you have been navigating life with an undiagnosed developmental condition in a world not attuned to your needs. I'm betting you haven't done a bad job of this already, although I also guess you can't see that at the moment.

ADHD is one of a number of neurodevelopmental disorders that affects how people focus and behave. And let me get this out now—I hate the word disorder! It has such negative connotations, making it sound as if there is something wrong with you or I, when there is nothing wrong with us!

ADHD impacts the functioning in the parts of our brains that controls attention, executive functioning and organisation. The exact causes of this are not fully known, though research shows that genetics play a big part. So, if you have a parent or grandparent with ADHD, you are more likely to have it too. There may also be links to brain injury, environmental risks (such as pollutants, parents smoking or alcohol use) during pregnancy, though the jury is still out on those. One thing's for sure: ADHD is *not* caused by poor diet, too much screen time, too much sugar, bad parenting or other external factors such as poverty or a chaotic family life.

Another thing we know is that boys are more likely to be diagnosed with ADHD than girls. But why is this? It's been hypothesised that this is due to how each gender presents its ADHD symptoms. Boys and men tend to be more hyperactive, externalising their symptoms. Whereas girls and women tend to be more inattentive and are more likely to internalise their symptoms. For example, a lack of concentration in a classroom or at work may be displayed by men and boys through fidgeting, being disruptive or constantly being on the go. Whereas, for women and girls it may present itself as forgetfulness, daydreaming or being easily distracted.

It's important to note that ADHD symptoms do not always match these gender stereotypes, so it could be that your symptoms are more externalised than internalised. Your symptoms might be more externalised rather than internalised, or they may have been more noticeable in childhood but overlooked because you were a girl at a time when ADHD was primarily associated with boys. ADHD symptoms and diagnoses is something we'll discuss in more detail in the first chapter.

In addition to symptoms and diagnosis, we'll also take a look at how hormones impact female ADHDers throughout their lifecycle. Other things to consider are the links between ADHD, memory, time, emotional regulation, burnout and the impact these have on our relationships and our work lives

So why read this book now? The answer is simple. Now is the right time because you have been struggling long enough and it's time to bring a stop to your struggle. Yes, there is medication that can help reduce the impact of ADHD symptoms. However, there is no 'cure' in the traditional sense. "Pills don't teach skills" and that's why implementing what you will learn in this book is incredibly important.

In fact, this book is the book I wish I'd had at the beginning of my ADHD journey. In 2021, after 22 years in the army, followed by 3 years studying to be a mental health nurse, I found myself in another new city, starting a new career as a mental health nurse. Something I had strived for since well before starting my degree. I was in a relationship with someone I loved very much (and vice versa). On the outside, life seemed pretty perfect. However, inside was a very different story.

I was getting more and more forgetful. The slightest additional change to my day would lead to massive overwhelm and emotional outbursts. My brain was foggy and my mood sank to the lowest it had ever been. I was crying (in secret) at the drop of a hat. I was terrified I was getting early onset dementia (I was only 44 at the time). I was literally going to work and then hiding away at home, isolating myself from everybody, not wanting them to see that I was struggling. My mood got so low that one day, whilst out with my gorgeous sprocker spaniel, Spud, I began to think about what was the point of being alive anymore. It was this thought that scared the shit out of me that made me go and see my GP.

My GP did some blood tests that showed I was anaemic, extremely low in vitamin D and also possibly in perimenopause. Great, I thought, some hormone replacement therapy (HRT), iron tablets and a bit of vitamin D and I'll be all sorted. Nope, there was going to be another twist to my tale...the medication helped alleviate the extreme symptoms I was experiencing, however, it was as if a switch had been flipped. While the symptoms improved, they didn't disappear entirely and I still struggled to cope. The silver lining for me during that time was that I no longer thought about ending my life.

A couple of months after that I started working at a university mental health and wellbeing team. Here I was, coming across plenty of students diagnosed with ADHD. Prior to then, I'd never come across ADHD before, apart from my friends' children. I didn't know anything about it, other than what I now know to be common misconceptions, such as "only naughty boys have ADHD" or "you grow out of it" or "you can't have ADHD if you are clever/got a good job/etc. or "everyone's got a little bit ADHD" or "ADHD is just an excuse for people who are lazy and lack willpower" and so on and so on. Through talking to the students and listening to their struggles around studying and 'adulting', I could see similarities to how I had secretly felt all of my life. I became curious about whether this was what had 'been wrong' with me all my life. Was it ADHD, or was I just a shit, lazy, useless person as my brain would tell me a lot of the time?

What are your thoughts about ADHD?

I've had to eat a lot of humble pie over the last couple of years since I started to wonder if ADHD was a thing for me. I have spent a lifetime secretly believing that it was due to bad parenting, an excuse for being lazy, something that could be fixed with a good bit of discipline, etc. Don't worry, the irony of me now writing a book on the subject is absolutely not lost on me.

Now that I know what I know, I often wonder how I did not know that I was an ADHDer for over 40 years of my life when it now seems so obvious to me. Maybe you are wondering the same too? Don't worry, you are not alone and once you start looking, you'll find that there are plenty of us out there.

To be fair to my parents, ADHD wasn't even a thing when I was growing up—never mind when *they* were growing up—so it's no wonder they didn't have a clue. My parents were born in the 1950s. My dad, who was born in 1950, definitely has undiagnosed ADHD. He admits this himself. Growing up, he had all the typical symptoms and, thanks to the education system back then, he was physically punished and left school without any formal qualifications. He has believed, for nearly all of his life, that he is just plain stupid.

ADHD is not a new condition. The earliest record of ADHD-type symptoms goes all the way back to the 1700s, though some say Hippocrates had mentioned a patient who could not keep their focus on anything. Knowing this, would you believe that in the UK, ADHD was only recognised as a valid condition in the year 2000 and not even officially recognised in adults till 2008?

Another thing is, girls are believed to be diagnosed with ADHD at just under half the rate of boys. However, when it comes to getting diagnosed in adulthood, women and men are diagnosed at the same rate. ADHD in women is often overlooked due to a lack of understanding about its different presentations in girls and women. Many women often receive their diagnosis after their child has been diagnosed. It's during the assessment process for their child that they recognise their own ADHD symptoms.

ADHD in women can go unseen for many years due to the long list of expectations society puts on women, such as believing that all women should know how to proficiently juggle managing themselves and their career alongside a home and a family. Whilst this can be a struggle for any woman, women with ADHD will often mask symptoms and problems in an attempt to conform to these expectations. Many women with ADHD internalise feelings of shame and guilt due to their struggles. They think, "Everyone else can do it, so why can't I?" This has a detrimental effect on their self-worth and self-esteem. I have yet to meet a woman diagnosed later in life who hasn't felt like she was failing as an adult, woman, mother, sister, daughter, etc., despite outward success in these areas.

The frustrating part is that women who are struggling with unrecognised ADHD symptoms will go to their doctor and come away with a diagnosis of anxiety or depression. Others will end up with diagnoses of bipolar disorder or personality disorder. Why is this? It could be for a number of reasons, though the lack of education for GP's on ADHD is an obvious factor. (Don't get me started on the lack of education on women's health as a whole.) Gender stereotyping doesn't help, but when a woman seeks support it will usually be based on symptoms related to mood and emotional regulation. All of which are also symptoms of mental health conditions. Treatment then becomes about symptom management rather than considering that the woman in question may be struggling due to undiagnosed ADHD. Though in defence of GPs (and to complicate matters further), there are several mental health conditions that can coexist with ADHD, making adult diagnosis even more challenging.

There is a lot of stigma around an ADHD diagnosis, especially as an adult. There are people who, despite a vast amount of evidence to the contrary, still do not believe ADHD is a proper medical condition (yes, I know, I was one of them). There is still a belief that having ADHD means you are stupid or that you will not succeed in life. When women do 'come out' as having ADHD, some people may think that they are lying or using it as a way to get out of things they don't want to do. Others believe that ADHD is a condition exclusive to boys and men, so a woman with ADHD must have something seriously wrong with her.

When I told my dad I was going in for an ADHD assessment, like a lot of others of his generation I've come across, he was quite confused. By that time, he had already begun to think that he may have ADHD, thanks to my best friend's sons who have all got diagnoses of ADHD and present very typically. However, how could *I* have ADHD? I had a successful 22-year career in the British Army, received an MBE and later earned a first-class honours degree in mental health nursing. Due to his understanding of ADHD, he struggled to understand that it is not tied to intelligence. My dad is far from unintelligent; he was a talented draughtsman and is a very skilled carpenter. Yet, because this involved apprenticeships and manual labour rather than academic study, to this day he will tell you that this does not count.

As mentioned, due to this stigma around ADHD, lots of girls and women will learn to "mask" their symptoms. Masking refers to behaviours people adopt to conform to socially accepted norms, especially in environments where it may not be safe to express their true selves. Ways in which ADHDers can mask can vary widely. For instance, some may stay very quiet and carefully choose their words (to counteract a tendency to talk excessively or blurt out inappropriate remarks). Others may obsessively check their belongings (to compensate for frequent losses), or learn to react in socially expected ways rather than expressing their true emotions (due to perceptions of overreacting). Some may become perfectionists as a response to disorganisation, among other strategies.

Many undiagnosed ADHD individuals are unaware that they're masking their symptoms. I certainly didn't recognise it in myself. All I could see around me while growing up were people that seemed to have their shit together—and I was not one of them. I learnt ways to make sure that others didn't see what a mess my life really was. I was trying to fit into a world that wasn't made for me to fit into and I didn't even know this. I thought I was the only one who was like this. Everyone else seemed "normal'. Honestly, thanks to my diagnosis, I now know that there is no such thing as "normal", and that there are so many more people out there who are like me.

I am not fully unmasked and I'm not sure I ever will be, although I work towards it every day. After spending so long not knowing who I was, it is a tricky task to unpick which of my behaviours is masking and which is not. So far, I can see how I avoided having visitors because of how embarrassed I was about my messy home, how I meticulously planned and documented everything to avoid forgetting and how I kept others at a distance to hide "the real me". I became fiercely independent, rarely seeking help and positioned myself to appear competent while secretly fearing being exposed as a complete fuck-up. The list goes on...

The easiest parts to identify for me are when I've hit burnout. Masking demands significant physical and mental energy to maintain the coping strategies that hide our differences and struggles from others. This is also what I believe led to earlier diagnoses of anxiety and depression.

You may be thinking that my ADHD symptoms can't be that bad if I have managed to write a book. Please don't let the fact that this book is in your hands fool you into thinking that this was an easy task for me. Every day, I have to use what I write about in this book to hack my ADHD brain. For example, if it were not for the accountability of working with Chloë and the team at Inspired By Publishing, this book would still just be an idea floating around my brain with all of the others I have on a daily basis. Each chapter has been written on the day of the deadline, despite having a whole week (sometimes two) to get it done. There have been more weeks that I care to count where I struggled to motivate myself to keep going after the initial excitement had worn off. I could never have done this without learning about my ADHD brain.

There is a common saying that goes, "If you've met one person with ADHD, you've met one person". ADHD affects us all in very different ways and ADHDers come in all shapes and sizes. The symptoms I struggle with may not be the same as yours. I can't remember who it was, but I heard someone once described it as being like a graphic equaliser. Imagine each symptom having their own slider, controlling its strength and impact. Individually, all of our sliders will be set at different levels to other ADHDers. This does not make us any more or less ADHD than anyone else, it just means we all have different challenges.

The great thing about all of this is that, once we identify our own particular challenges, we can learn to manage *them*, rather than them managing *us*.

I absolutely believe that every ADHDer on this planet does not need to feel broken. That they do not need to feel alone or that they are shit women, wives, or mothers. That we all have amazing gifts to give to the world, regardless of what has happened to us before or the fact that our brains are wired differently to others.

Yes, even you!

I know, without even meeting you, that you have already achieved so much despite undiagnosed ADHD, and once you learn about what it is that will help your unique brain, you're going to be unstoppable.

Chapter 1
WTF is ADHD?

"ADHD is the diabetes of psychology. It's a chronic disorder that must be managed every day to prevent the secondary harms it's going to cause... ADHD is the most treatable disorder in psychiatry... The biggest problem is, most people don't get treatment."
– Dr. Russel A. Barkey

Let's jump straight in and begin by understanding what ADHD is—and perhaps more crucially, what it isn't. ADHD is a lifelong neurodevelopmental condition that affects our attention, decision-making processes and actions. It also influences our emotional regulation. ADHD is also genetic. It is not caused by bad parenting, bad diet, bad health, poverty or any other external factor. However, in all honesty, they don't help. Most importantly, no two ADHDers are the same when it comes to how their symptoms affect them.

When I suspected I had ADHD, I had so many questions. The only information I had was based on the stereotype of young boys with ADHD. I had never met an adult with ADHD—or so I thought. Looking back, I realise I've been surrounded by people with ADHD for most of my life. I just didn't know what I was looking for.

The information out there can be confusing when you first start looking into ADHD. So, in this book, I'm going to keep it simple. Not because I doubt your intelligence, but because that's how I find it easier to understand it.

While the term "deficit" is commonly associated with ADHD, the reality is quite different. ADHDers don't lack attention; rather, we often have too much of it and struggle with maintaining focus.

For instance, have you ever found yourself in a busy coffee shop or restaurant where multiple conversations are competing for your attention? You might effortlessly tune into nearby details, like a couple discussing holiday plans or friends sharing their recent experiences. Yet, despite this heightened awareness, concentrating on a book becomes challenging, leading to repeated page flipping or difficulty staying engaged in the conversation with the person you are with. Similarly, you might multitask while watching TV, simultaneously scrolling through your phone and chatting with a friend on WhatsApp. Suddenly, you become captivated by an actor whose face seems familiar, but whose name escapes you, prompting a detour into Google searches or asking your viewing companion for assistance, often to their frustration.

The Three Types of ADHD

To better understand these experiences, it's important to know that there are three different types of ADHD: inattentive type, hyperactive-impulsive type and combined type. Assessments look at all of the symptoms of ADHD, scoring you based on how many symptoms you exhibit in the inattentive and hyperactive-impulsive categories. If you score high in both, you receive a diagnosis of combined type ADHD.

Inattentive Type

ADHD, particularly the inattentive type, presents with a range of symptoms. These include making careless mistakes or lacking attention to detail, experiencing difficulty in sustaining attention and sometimes being unable to listen when spoken to directly. Individuals might also struggle to follow through on tasks and instructions, exhibit poor organisational skills and avoid or dislike tasks requiring sustained mental effort. They may frequently lose items necessary for tasks or activities and find themselves easily distracted, such as during a maths exam. Additionally, forgetfulness in daily activities is common among those with this type of ADHD.

Hyperactive-Impulsive Type

On the other hand, hyperactive-impulsive type ADHD involves distinct behaviours. This includes fidgeting with or tapping hands or feet, frequently leaving one's seat when remaining seated is expected, experiencing restlessness and finding it challenging to engage in quiet activities. Individuals with this type may seem constantly "on-the-go" or as if "driven by a motor," talk excessively, blurt out answers, struggle with waiting their turn and may interrupt or intrude on others.

Combined Type

As the name suggests, this is a combination of both hyperactive-impulsive and inattentive type ADHD. I'm of the combined type; my ADHD assessment is probably the highest I've ever scored on a test. At the time, I didn't know whether to celebrate due to the high score or be embarrassed. Now, I totally celebrate it!

Should I Get A Diagnosis?

If you haven't got a diagnosis already and are wondering if you truly need one, my advice is always the same: "It's up to you". Getting diagnosed is a very personal decision and will have a different impact on your life than it has on mine. If a diagnosis offers clarity and support, then it's worth considering. Personally, I went through the diagnosis process for a couple of reasons: Self-diagnosis was not enough to calm the negative voice in my head telling me I was lazy and not as good as everyone else. I doubted my self-diagnosis, and I was also curious about the diagnosis process. Additionally, I knew that I could access additional support at work and in my studies. Most of all, I have always wanted to start my own business, but despite this desire, I just could not "make myself" do what I needed to fulfil this dream. If it was ADHD getting in the way, I wanted to know if medication would help.

What are the Advantages and Disadvantages of Getting Diagnosed?

There is no clear-cut answer to this question. As with much of what is contained within this book, this is something only you can answer, depending on your personal circumstances. In this section, I'll talk about the advantages and disadvantages either I have experienced or those I have worked with or spoken to have experienced:

The Good Stuff

A diagnosis can give you clarity and an explanation for things you may have struggled with throughout your life, such as attention, organisation and emotional regulation. This can be extremely validating, leading to greater self-compassion and self-acceptance.

With the right interventions, whether medical treatment through medication or non-medicinal support via coaching or therapy, adults with ADHD can learn coping strategies and mechanisms to help manage their symptoms. This can lead to improvements at work, within relationships and in overall quality of life.

Knowing you have ADHD can help you access ADHD-specific support such as coaching, therapy and support groups. It can also help with getting accommodations (reasonable adjustments) within education and work settings. Becoming part of the ADHD community has been liberating for me and many other women I know. Together we support each other, and while our struggles are different, we don't have to explain ourselves. We just know.

Openly discussing ADHD can help educate others about the condition and challenge negative stereotypes. This can aid understanding and acceptance within personal and professional relationships. I'm sure people in my life are tired of me talking about ADHD, however, I'm not going to stop. The more I talk about it, the more people will know they are not alone.

Lastly, ADHD can sometimes occur with other mental health conditions, such as anxiety or depression. A diagnosis of ADHD can lead to getting the right treatment for these conditions if required.

What People Don't Realise...

Getting a diagnosis in adulthood can be a complex and emotional experience, bringing up feelings of frustration, grief or anger (see "The Diagnosis Rollercoaster" below for more on this).

The process of getting a diagnosis can be time-consuming and expensive, involving several processes, appointments and hours completing what can feel like a mountain of paperwork. Consideration also needs to be made about the financial aspect of treatment options such as coaching, therapy and medication.

Unfortunately, despite increasing awareness, there is still a lot of stigma around ADHD. ADHDers may experience negative attitudes or misunderstandings from others in their lives.

Medication can be highly effective for managing ADHD symptoms, but it can also come with side effects that require regular monitoring and adjustment. For some people, medication may not be appropriate due to other health concerns or because it just doesn't work for them.

Navigating ADHD in relationships can be complex, whether or not the other partner is neurodiverse. Partners and family members may also need time to adjust to any diagnosis and its implications for all concerned.

Ultimately, you must weigh up the advantages and disadvantages of pursuing an ADHD diagnosis based on your personal circumstances. I would always advise speaking to a suitably qualified therapist or healthcare professional if you are considering a diagnosis, as they can help you navigate the process and provide support as needed.

When thinking about assessments or diagnosis, there are a couple of routes you can take depending on your current situation and desired final outcome. The routes open to everyone are medical diagnosis and self-diagnosis.

Where Should I Start?

To get a diagnosis of ADHD as an adult in the UK you can either choose to go private or via the NHS. If you choose to go private, you will have to pay for this and it is not cheap. Waiting lists are generally shorter than the NHS, but be aware that private diagnoses are increasingly not being recognised by GPs for ongoing medication prescriptions, which may leave you having to pay private prescription prices moving forward.

A good place to start is with a screening tool, which can be easily found online. They are very easy to fill in and, while they do not diagnose you with ADHD, they can indicate whether further exploration is warranted. Printing off the results and taking them to your GP appointment can be a great way to start the conversation.

Speaking to Your GP

At the time of writing, GP's do not diagnose ADHD in the UK. However, they are the gatekeepers to further assessment. Depending on your GP, it can prove difficult to get past this stage and you may need to do a lot of homework before speaking to them, especially as a woman. The sad fact is that GPs receive very little training on ADHD, and what training they may have had often relates to the stereotype of young boys who are disruptive in school.

Prepare yourself by bringing a completed screening tool and writing down the symptoms you are concerned about, with relevant examples, so you do not forget anything during your appointment. Despite bringing this information when I spoke to my GP, she still made me complete another screening tool via their own surgery system. This seemed a bit silly to me but I was happy to do it as I felt very lucky that my GP 'believed' me and did not question my request for further assessment. Unfortunately, I've met a lot of women who have had to fight for an assessment.

If you do find that your GP is a bit of an arse and either refuses to refer you for an assessment or they add more obstacles in your way, please don't give up. Remember, you're made of stronger stuff. You've made it through the whole of your life so far with undiagnosed ADHD, in a world that wasn't made for your brain. Don't let an ignorant dickhead get in the way of you getting what you need. You may need to go home and have a cry or a tantrum (personally, I love a bit of both). Once this is done, dust yourself down like the warrior you are and ask to see a different GP in your surgery. One helpful tip is to ask the receptionist which GP is better with neurodiversity.

Referral and Assessment

If your GP decides that a referral is appropriate, they will make a referral to the local adult ADHD service.

Assessments are carried out by a psychiatrist, psychologist or specialist ADHD nurse. They may include:

- Interviews with you to discuss your childhood experiences, current concerns and family history.

- Interviews with people close to you (or more often questionnaires), such as partners, parents or close friends, to get a broader perspective.

- Cognitive tests to assess attention, memory and executive functioning.

- Physical examination to rule out other medical conditions that could be causing similar symptoms.

One common concern for adults without anyone in their lives who can comment on their childhood is figuring out who can fill in the family/partner/friend form. I had that worry too, as I don't really have close family or a partner. Instead, I chose a work colleague who sees me regularly and has also spoken to me about how she could see ADHD traits in me before I decided to go for an assessment. She could not comment on my childhood, of course, but there wasn't anyone else in my life that could, so that information is missing regardless. This was not a problem.

Diagnosis and Treatment

Based on the assessment and all the information gathered, the specialist will determine whether you meet the criteria for an ADHD diagnosis. If you are diagnosed, they will discuss treatment options, which may include medication or some form of psychoeducation/therapy such as ADHD coaching or behavioural therapies.

When it comes to getting a diagnosis, you may encounter several barriers, your GP being one of them. Be prepared as much as possible, be persistent and be ready to advocate for yourself. Find places where you can talk to others and seek support from those who have been through the process. There are many online and in-person support groups, some of which I will share at the end of the book.

Self-Diagnosis

This refers to the act of identifying symptoms and characteristics in yourself that align with the diagnostic criteria for ADHD, without going through a formal assessment by an ADHD specialist. Due to the length of waiting lists, self-diagnosis is one way of starting to access the support that may help you with the symptoms you are experiencing. As an ADHD coach, I do not require people to have a formal diagnosis. Additionally, you can still get work-related support via the Government Access to Work Scheme without a diagnosis.

While self-diagnosis can be valid, it is important to recognise that there are limitations to it. For one, a number of mental and physical health conditions share symptoms with ADHD. Misdiagnosing yourself could lead to you not getting the right treatment or accessing inappropriate support/treatment. Also, many ADHDers also live with mental health conditions such as anxiety and depression. Only a trained professional can help you understand whether these symptoms are part of ADHD or another condition.

Ultimately, seeking professional help is essential for ensuring proper diagnosis and access to appropriate treatment and support. Rather than relying solely on self-diagnosis, maybe consider speaking to your GP or a mental health professional. They can assess your symptoms and provide accurate information about ADHD, moving towards a formal diagnosis if needed.

If you decide to go for an assessment, while waiting, you could focus on self-management of your symptoms through learning effective coping strategies. The tools and techniques mentioned in this book are a great place to start.

The Diagnosis Rollercoaster

The process of getting an ADHD diagnosis in adulthood is often likened to the stages of grief. These stages are shock and denial; anger; bargaining; depression and acceptance. As with grief, this is not a linear experience where we move smoothly from one stage to another, which is why you may also hear it referred to as the "ADHD diagnosis rollercoaster".

I really resonate with the idea of it being a rollercoaster and the link to the stages of grief. At the beginning I did not believe it at all, there was no way I had ADHD. It came as a bit of a shock to me. Then the deeper I went down the rabbit hole, the more I could see all of the symptoms throughout my life. I then started to doubt if I was making things up to try and fit the diagnostic criteria and make excuses for areas in my life where I felt like a failure. I experienced a lot of denial. I felt huge imposter syndrome, even right up to the moment my psychiatrist confirmed that I had ADHD. I remember feeling so unsettled and worried I had spent the last year believing it was ADHD, and I was just about to be told it wasn't, that I had to pick up my laptop and pace around the room while he was giving me my assessment results. The relief I felt on hearing that it was ADHD was immense. However, that was not the end of my rollercoaster, as I've been up and down those tracks many times (so far).

I have had small bouts of anger but the biggest emotion I have felt since finding out about ADHD is sadness. I have experienced sadness (and at times still do) when I think about some parts of my life that I may have missed out on, such as having children, closer relationships with friends and family and missed opportunities. All of these have led me to wonder whether things may have been different had I been diagnosed earlier and received the appropriate treatment.

These days, I find myself mostly in acceptance and feeling quite grateful that I finally know what it is. For once, the negative voice in my head is quiet. The voice that told me I am 'a failure, a bad adult, terrible partner, awful friend' and so much more, is quiet (most of the time).

Advocate for Yourself Within the Healthcare System

Unfortunately, there will be times when you have to advocate for yourself throughout this process. The system is not ADHD-friendly at all. In fact, it is quite the opposite, so it helps to be prepared.

Gather Information

Document your symptoms, their severity and how they impact your daily life. If you have access to childhood stories or school reports, gather that information too. This may be a struggle, as it's exactly the type of thing ADHDers find challenging. See if you can find a friend or loved one to help you. Take it in small chunks rather than feeling overwhelmed by how big the task feels. Chapter 4 provides some great tips on time management that will help.

Express Your Concerns Clearly

Explain how your symptoms interfere with different aspects of your life, such as work, relationships and overall well-being. We often downplay how things affect us for fear of being judged, or because we have been masking for so long that we're not sure of our symptoms and struggles. You may want to write a script or some notes for when you speak to your GP or assessor. Describe your worst days, weeks or situations—those times when you really can't cope.

Ask Questions and Do Your Research
Knowledge is power. Don't be afraid to ask other ADHDers how ADHD affects them. Find forums or groups where you can connect with others. Look at national ADHD charities and groups. You may find that you have more information on ADHD than your GP does. Don't be afraid to let them know this. Remember, they get very little training on ADHD.

Don't Be Afraid to Ask for a Second Opinion
If you are not satisfied with the answers you're getting, ask to consult with another healthcare professional.

Diagnosis is Just One Piece of the Puzzle
The real journey begins after diagnosis, as you start to understand how ADHD affects you, learn coping strategies that work for you and find a support system.

Medication can help manage some ADHD symptoms, however, there is no cure. As the saying goes, "Pills don't teach skills". Psychoeducation and ADHD coaching are really helpful for learning more about how ADHD shows up in your life, developing self-awareness, identifying your strengths and exploring the skills you need to thrive. One way to look at it is that medication can help quieten the engine, but coaching teaches you how to drive.

The journey to diagnosis and beyond can be challenging, but remember, while at times it may seem as if you are alone, I promise you that you are not.

Chapter 2
Hormones and ADHD

"When hormones play up, they distort your whole vision. You don't have to withdraw to a cave, but you must be able to see through this."
– Sadhguru

Does it feel like your ADHD symptoms worsen at particular times of the month? And, if you're taking ADHD medication, does it not work as well as it normally does? Some days you feel great. You're on time for work and finish your to-do list. But on other days, you're back to putting your car keys in the fridge and the smallest thing sparks off a crippling feeling of failure, otherwise known as Rejection Sensitive Dysphoria (RSD).

We know that ADHD looks different for female ADHDers. We also know that our moods change due to our monthly cycles. However, what about our ADHD symptoms? At the time of writing this book (2024), there is a massive gap in research when it comes to women's health. New research shows that women are underrepresented in clinical trials. Also, research proposed by women, for women, receives less funding than research proposed by men, for men. There remains gender inequality in healthcare (alongside pay and education—but don't get me started on those as this will end up a whole different book).

But the lack of formal research doesn't mean there is no information. There is data on how hormones impact women with ADHD at different life stages. While I know many of you reading this will be past some of these stages, I thought it was important to look at them all, starting in childhood. Not only will this give you more insight into what may have been going on for you when you were younger, but it also provides information you can share with any younger female ADHDers in your life. I'm quite embarrassed to admit that it wasn't until after 45 years of life that I started to understand what had been going on in my body for decades. If I had known even the basics about hormones while growing up, even without the addition of ADHD symptoms, I know my life would have been so much easier.

Hormonal changes are believed to be linked to fluctuations in ADHD symptoms in girls and women.

This has all been anecdotal until a study published at the beginning of 2024 confirmed what many female ADHDers already knew: Hormones can really fuck about with our ADHD symptoms and medication. This is why the information within this chapter is important. If we become aware of how our hormones impact our symptoms and medication, rather than feel we are a slave to our hormones, we can take control and make plans to lessen the impact. Without this awareness, our hormones run rampant over us, taking control, and the more we are impacted by our symptoms, the harder our lives get. I wish I'd known this when I was a hell of a lot younger because all of the tips at the end of the chapter can benefit women and girls of all ages and stages.

While exploring my ADHD diagnosis, I have been lucky enough to meet many women who have learned to successfully navigate the fluctuations in hormones and ADHD symptoms, meaning they are hardly impacted anymore. How have they done this? By educating themselves and becoming aware of their cycles and the differences they feel throughout.

What about ADHDers who have had hysterectomies? Are they impacted by all of this too? The short answer is yes. For those who also have their ovaries removed, they go straight into menopause. Those who retain one or both ovaries are more likely to go into menopause earlier but will still have a regular cycle just as before, although it will become trickier to monitor as there will not be a period due to the absence of a womb. This is where I've struggled when it comes to monitoring my cycle. When I was 31, I had a hysterectomy due to endometriosis. I kept my ovaries, which meant that I continued to have a cycle, but with no monthly bleed, I never knew where I was in that cycle. That is, until more recently when I started to take more notice of my ADHD symptoms. Now, when I start to trip over things, bump into things and become less coordinated, I know I'm at the part of my cycle where oestrogen is low, which tells me that I need to slow down and take it easy for a couple of days.

My friend has the monitoring of her cycle down to a fine art. She plans her months and weeks around it, so when she is low on oestrogen, her diary is less busy than during the days/weeks when she knows she will have more energy and focus and can manage her ADHD symptoms better. Initially, she was frustrated at having to force herself to take it slower at times during her cycle, but now she can see (and feel) the benefits of this.

Hormones and ADHD

Hormones are like little messengers, carrying information through our bodies and turning systems on and off as they go. In females, oestrogen and progesterone regulate processes related to puberty and childbirth. However, they also control the chemical processes in our brains that impact mood, energy and yep, you've guessed it—ADHD symptoms.

The two main hormones affecting our ADHD symptoms are oestrogen and progesterone. Think of oestrogen as the key that unlocks happiness, satisfaction and thinking by releasing the "happy hormones": dopamine, serotonin and norepinephrine. Progesterone triggers the release of GABA, which calms our nervous systems.

While this sounds amazing on paper, for the ADHD brain that needs dopamine, GABA acts like a depressant. It takes away all the good stuff oestrogen gives us, worsening brain fog, irritability, sadness, fatigue and making inattention even worse. We become unregulated, and our executive functioning goes out of the window.

ADHD, Childhood and Puberty

At birth, our oestrogen and progesterone levels are high, but they drop to very low, consistent levels after a few months. For some girls, their ADHD symptoms start to become apparent during childhood. If ADHD is recognised before puberty, due to the consistency in hormone levels, it is easier to treat and that treatment looks very similar to that of boys.

When a girl starts puberty there is a rapid increase of both oestrogen and progesterone. Both have sharply risen. But, progesterone often cancels out the benefits of oestrogen. This can increase levels of anxiety, depression, impulsivity and irritability, making ADHD symptoms even harder to manage. As if that isn't bad enough, rising hormone levels often make medication less effective, and a higher dose doesn't always help.

Oestrogen and progesterone levels continue to rise until sometime into our twenties. However, the rise will also bring about dramatic changes. The levels will change throughout each of our menstrual cycles, causing energy, mood and ADHD symptoms to change.

ADHD Symptoms and the Menstrual Cycle

For the first two weeks of our cycles, oestrogen levels peak. This can boost our mood and energy. Our ADHD symptoms can be easier to manage during this time. Over the next two weeks, progesterone levels rise, oestrogen levels start to drop. This is when we may notice a decline in our mood and energy. ADHD symptoms can become more troublesome, and for some, unmanageable. As our period starts, both oestrogen and progesterone levels drop and the cycle begins anew.

ADHD and Pregnancy

It's fascinating how a woman's body adapts during pregnancy, especially regarding hormonal changes. During the first trimester, there's a significant increase in both oestrogen and progesterone levels, which can bring about challenges like fatigue, mood fluctuations and heightened anxiety. Additionally, ADHD symptoms may become more noticeable. Doctors often recommend discontinuing stimulant medication during this time, which might seem daunting initially. However, as the pregnancy progresses into the second and third trimesters, the body's steady and elevated oestrogen levels often work wonders in alleviating ADHD symptoms and stabilising mood swings. It's like a natural remedy. After childbirth, there might be a resurgence of challenges as oestrogen and progesterone levels drop. However, with the right support and awareness, all of these transitions can be managed effectively.

ADHD, Perimenopause and Menopause

Perimenopause usually starts in our mid forties, however, this can be earlier for some. This stage can last about ten years. During this time, oestrogen and progesterone levels become erratic and drop often. This also causes a drop in the happy hormones. This leads to low mood, tiredness, brain fog, forgetfulness, inattentiveness and irritability. And this is for those without ADHD!

For ADHDers who already have difficulties with those symptoms, perimenopause can be an especially tough time. Menopause officially begins twelve months after your last period, with a significant drop in oestrogen levels. The good news is that progesterone levels also drop, allowing any remaining oestrogen to be more effective. As hormones stop cycling, treatment becomes easier because symptoms are more consistent.

Perimenopause is what pushed me over the edge. It made it hard to manage what I now know to be undiagnosed ADHD. Until then, I didn't know I was working hard to cover for my executive function difficulties. I had enough energy to keep myself contained and hide the real me. That all stopped when perimenopause hit! While it felt awful at the time, I am grateful that the hormonal shifts led to the mask falling off. Knowing myself better, I am becoming who I was all along and helping others through this book and coaching late-diagnosed ADHDers.

Managing Changing Hormones When You Have ADHD

Okay, so basically all we have to do when it comes to managing our ADHD symptoms as women is wait for menopause...I'm kidding! Managing ADHD symptoms as women can be tricky due to fluctuating hormones, but there are strategies we can do to help.

Cycle Tracking

Cycle tracking can help you predict your symptoms and make plans to combat them. By tracking your cycle, you can learn to plan around the peaks and troughs of energy, mood and ADHD symptoms. For example, you can lighten your workload when you know you will have little energy, or work a bit harder at regulating your emotions and RSD when your hormones begin to drop. You will also know when your symptoms are due to improve. Now, I know what you are thinking and yes, I know that as ADHDers we struggle with keeping track of things. Thankfully, many phone and watch apps can help with this.

Diet and Exercise

Diet and exercise can significantly impact the fluctuations of female hormones and ADHD symptoms. Specific foods can positively influence hormone balance, and there's a growing trend of trainers and nutritionists specialising in supporting women ADHDers. Incorporating a balanced diet and a regular exercise routine not only helps alleviate ADHD symptoms, but also serves to regulate hormones as well.

Coaching

Tailored coaching, whether for ADHD, menopause or hormonal and lifestyle issues, offers comprehensive support for managing the fluctuations of female hormones and ADHD symptoms. More and more coaches are starting to specialise in these areas, providing strategies and support systems tailored to address these dual challenges.

Medication

In addition to ADHD medication, the use of hormone replacement therapy (HRT) and antidepressants alongside ADHD medication can effectively address mood fluctuations and ADHD symptoms. However, this will vary from person to person, so consulting a healthcare professional for personalised advice is essential.

Psychotherapy

Psychotherapy aids in addressing executive functioning challenges and mood regulation, and is particularly crucial for women navigating late-diagnosed ADHD and hormonal changes. Many ADHDers also grapple with years of low self-esteem, self-confidence issues and negative self-perceptions, making therapy vital for exploration and healing.

Mindfulness

Mindfulness practices further benefit ADHDers by enhancing emotional regulation and overall well-being. Through practices like deep breathing and body scans, mindfulness cultivates present-moment awareness, enabling individuals to observe their emotions without impulsively reacting. This heightened awareness builds resilience to stress and promotes a sense of inner calm, ultimately enhancing emotional regulation and overall well-being.

Psychoeducation

Finally, psychoeducation empowers ADHDers to better understand and manage the fluctuations of female hormones and ADHD symptoms. Understanding these conditions and their effects can provide valuable insights into developing effective coping strategies and self-care routines tailored to your unique needs.

Discovering ADHD later in life while navigating hormonal changes can be challenging, but it also opens doors to understanding yourself in new ways. Remember, your journey is unique, and every step you take towards managing both your ADHD and your hormones is a testament to your resilience. You're not alone in this journey, and each day brings new opportunities for growth and self-discovery. I know you've got this!

Believe in yourself, remain curious, and trust in your ability to overcome any obstacle that comes your way. And if all else fails, remember that a sweet treat and a good laugh works wonders!

Chapter 3
Beyond Forgetfulness

*"ADHD clearly appears to be a problem of willpower failure,
but it is actually a problem with the interacting dynamics of
emotion, working memory and the chemistry of the brain."*
– Thomas E. Brown

Have you ever found yourself struggling to remember
where you put your keys, what you did last week or
even what someone just said to you in a conversation?
Maybe you've zoned out during an important meeting
or missed details in a task because your mind kept
jumping from one thing to another. I know I do this all
of the time. In this chapter, we'll look at how ADHD
affects memory and what we can do about it.

Memory is crucial for our daily functioning,
underpinning learning, problem-solving and our
relationships with others. For ADHDers, mastering
memory skills is particularly important, as it can
mitigate the impact of attentional struggles and

impulsivity. Without effective memory techniques, ADHDers face loads of challenges, from missing appointments and forgetting deadlines to underperforming at work. Such difficulties can lead to feelings of frustration, inadequacy and strain on relationships.

By learning how to hack our memory, ADHDers can improve their ability to retain information, fulfil responsibilities and stop getting in trouble for forgetting birthdays, anniversaries, to buy milk on the way home...and so much more!

First, a quick overview of what memory is and how it works. There are three types of memory: working memory, short-term memory and long-term memory. The memory process works like this: Immediate tasks are processed first and stored briefly in short-term memory.

More demanding memory tasks, such as remembering instructions long enough to complete a task, rely on working memory. Long-term memories form when something is emotionally charged or deemed important.

Memory and ADHD

ADHDers often have memory issues. Research suggests this happens because certain parts of their brains, which control focus, attention, distraction and memory, aren't as active as in people without ADHD.

ADHD can significantly impact working memory, crucial for retaining information long enough to act upon it. ADHDers commonly face various memory challenges, often forgetting household tasks like paying bills, struggling with the sequences of instructions, making careless mistakes due to a lack of attention to detail, losing important items such as keys or phones or even forgetting significant occasions like birthdays or anniversaries (a topic I'll delve into further in the relationship chapter).

Additionally, keeping track of deadlines and staying focussed during conversations or tasks can be quite tricky for ADHDers.

The different types of ADHD can have differing impacts on memory. ADHDers with the impulsive/hyperactive type do not struggle with attention. But, due to trouble staying still, they may miss information because they are always on the go. Inattentive type ADHDers struggle to focus and stay on task. Not paying attention creates problems, hindering the encoding of needed information for memory. Encoding is when the brain attaches meaning to an experience. If information isn't encoded properly, it won't be remembered, impairing long-term memory. People with combined type ADHD (like me) experience a combination of both sets of problems.

Memory and Perimenopause

Many women with late-diagnosed ADHD find themselves navigating not just the challenges of ADHD but also the onset of perimenopause. It's often this combination that pushes them to seek help from their doctors.

During perimenopause, many women experience what's commonly referred to as "brain fog". This foggy feeling can impact memory, motor skills, attention and the ability to focus on tasks.

While the exact reasons behind memory issues during perimenopause aren't fully understood, researchers believe that fluctuating hormones like oestrogen and progesterone play a significant role. The good news for non-ADHDers is that, for many, these symptoms tend to improve over time. Additionally, Hormone Replacement Therapy (HRT) may offer relief for those who can safely use it. For those of us whose ADHD symptoms have not become unmanageable, it's important that we learn how to "hack" our memory.

Looking back, I have always had challenges around my memory. Names, appointments and past events–all easily forgotten. However, I found ways of adapting. I avoided exams and wrote down instructions. I also deflected introductions to people whose names I could not remember. It wasn't ideal but it was manageable.

It all came to a head in October 2021. My memory was worse than ever. I could not concentrate. I was easily confused and overwhelmed. Words escaped me in the middle of sentences. My head felt constantly fuzzy, as if my brain was covered in cotton wool. Tasks I could do before became almost impossible, and my previous adaptations failed me nearly every time. I was 44 and terrified that I was at the start of early onset dementia.

HRT helped with the other symptoms of perimenopause and lifted the fog from my brain. But, the memory issues continued. This is when I thought there must be more to it. I had been introduced to ADHD while working in a university mental health team. That's when I started exploring ADHD as a possible cause.

Before we look at things that can help ADHDers with memory, it is very important to note that there is no evidence linking memory problems to intelligence.

Yes, ADHD can make learning and remembering information harder. But those of us with ADHD have the same potential as anyone else once we figure out what we need to perform at our best.

Tackle Memory Problems

Before we jump into this section, I want to acknowledge that we all work differently and that not all of my suggestions may work for you. That's perfectly okay. Keep the things that work, dump those that don't.

Externalise Your Thoughts

I've often thought, "I'll remember that," only to forget it completely. Sound familiar? It used to really bother me, feeling like I should remember everything. But getting upset didn't help; it just stressed me out more. What did help? Accepting that memory alone isn't reliable. Now, I use planners, reminder apps and notebooks to keep track. My smartwatch has become my "second brain" on my wrist.

Whenever I think of something important, I send a voice note to my reminder app. No more stress about remembering or worrying about forgetting. Although one con to this is that I have to make sure that all of my other watch notifications are switched off to avoid distractions.

Break It Down

Over recent years, I've found myself getting overwhelmed by big tasks. It's like I become paralysed when faced with doing them, making it really hard to get started. One way of overcoming this is to divide big tasks into smaller steps. This also helps to reduce the strain on your working memory.

You could also combine this technique with the use of a list to keep you on track. I understand that even breaking tasks into smaller chunks can be overwhelming, but nowadays, there are some great ADHD-friendly artificial intelligence (AI) apps that can do it for you.

Avoid Multitasking

How many times do we hear about how "women are great at multitasking"? Well, some of them might be, but I'm definitely not. If I'm multitasking, I'm basically half-arsing a number of different things. When we try to do more than one thing at a time, we increase our chances of making mistakes or forgetting something vitally important.

My advice is to try and resist the urge to multitask. To minimise distractions, keep only essential items nearby while you work. Close unnecessary tabs and apps on your computer and in your mind. Additionally, consider using apps and notification blockers on your phone to help maintain focus.

Location, Location, Location
Create spots for keys, wallet, phone or any other important day-to-day items. Use them and avoid the "put it down and forget it" cycle. This is still a work in progress for me. I'm great with my keys, not so good with my wallet. At home, my keys live by the front door. My wallet is generally in my bag, however, it's my phone that I lose the most.

There have been plenty of times where I've "lost" my phone, only to find it next to me when I ask my smartwatch to activate the location. After listening to a couple of podcasts, I've found that for some reason, the fridge is a popular location where ADHDers find missing items. So maybe next time you've lost something, have a look in the fridge first!

See It to Remember It
If I don't see it, it doesn't exist. Paired with my abysmal memory, it's a wonder I get anything done. I combat this by using visual aids such as checklists, colour

coding or mind maps to make information stick. Making it fun and interesting triggers our interest-based nervous system, making it more likely that we will take notice. I use whiteboards for this, dotted around my house. My friend, who is much more creative than I am, doesn't write what she needs to remember on her whiteboard–she draws it. For her, when it was written, she didn't notice it. However, now that whatever she had to remember is a picture, it makes a huge difference.

Routine is King

Establishing routines for daily tasks can be really helpful. Although it can be a bit of a love-hate scenario for many ADHDers. We know we need routines to thrive, but the idea of being tied to them can drive us a bit crazy. Routines are essential for reducing decision fatigue and freeing up mental bandwidth.

Take Albert Einstein, for example. He famously wore the same outfit every day, multiple versions of the same suit to avoid wasting brainpower on what to wear. While you don't need to go to that extreme, having consistent routines can work wonders for the ADHD brain.

Habit Stacking

If you keep forgetting something or want to start a new habit, try tying that habit to something you already do every day. For example, I wanted to meditate regularly but kept forgetting. Now, I do it while waiting for my morning coffee. When I make coffee, I know it's time to meditate. I still don't meditate everyday (and that's okay!), but I'm doing it much more often than I was when I first started.

Move Your Body
Research shows that exercise helps reduce ADHD symptoms. It also improves focus, memory and mood. Find activities that interest your nervous system. If they are enjoyable, then you're more likely to make them a habit.

Having Spud, my dog, really helps me with this. Unless I'm away from home and he's at the boarders, I have to get out of bed and go for a walk every morning–rain, hail or shine. Some days I may not like it, preferring to stay in bed. But I definitely notice the difference in my day when I haven't been out with him.

Prioritise Sleep
Sleep is one of the foundations for both our mental and physical health. When we sleep, our brain is storing any new learning and memories we've gained throughout the course of the day into our long term

memory. That's why sleep issues can make executive functioning even more difficult.

A well-rested brain is a sharper brain. Aim for consistent, quality sleep. If you struggle with this, there are a number of apps that can help.

One of my go-to things when I'm struggling to sleep is something called Yoga Nidra. Give it a Google, and you'll find plenty of recordings to give a go.

Be Kind to Yourself

I bang on about this all of the time and it is something I've historically been really shit at. Learning self compassion has been one of the greatest things I've done for myself. Focus on progress, not perfection. Celebrate small wins and don't beat yourself up for slip-ups. You are only human, after all.

Remember, memory problems can be particularly challenging symptoms for ADHDers. There are things that you can do to make it easier for you and improve your chances of success. By embracing the strategies and tips shared here for "hacking" memory, you're taking proactive steps towards a less stressful life. Each birthday remembered or trip to the shop and coming home with the right item, is a victory.

Keep experimenting with different techniques, stay patient with yourself and celebrate every success–no matter how small you think it is.

Chapter 4
Time Management and ADHD

*"Yesterday is gone. Tomorrow has yet to come. We only
have today. Let us begin."*
– Mother Teresa

Are you never on time, either late for everything or too
early? Do tasks take longer to complete than what you
initially thought they would? What about planning
ahead, is it almost impossible? Does it feel as if time is
just passing you by? Wondering why you just can't get
your shit together? This, my friend, is time blindness,
and I am yet to meet an ADHDer who does not struggle
with time in some way.

I'm sure I don't need to tell you why time management
is important, especially when you are bad at it. Maybe
there are enough people telling you this and you feel
bad enough already. Don't worry, this chapter is not

about making you feel any worse. It's about acknowledging the problem lots of ADHDers share and looking at how you can get better at it. However, I won't ever say it'll be a problem that can be completely solved, as we are human and there will still be times when we still fuck it up despite our best efforts.

Take me, for instance. I've always thought I was good with time. After over 2 decades in the army, I have been trained to never be late for anything. We were trained to be somewhere five minutes before the start time–*that* was being on time. So, to be extra sure we were on time, we had to be there five minutes before that. The consequences for being late were enough to trigger that lovely fear-based nervous system of mine.

However, the irony of all of this, especially when writing a chapter on time management, is that, midway through writing it, I had to send a voice note to my publisher to say it was going to be late. And here's why…

Time Management Hurdles for ADHDers

It's Either Now or Not Now

For many ADHDers, there are only 2 time zones: now or not now. This makes it hard to plan tasks, stick to goals, prioritise, remember things and overall, can just be really overwhelming.I can't count the times I've told myself to remember something, hoping this time it will stick, only to "go once around the fishbowl" and forget it entirely. Or I make plans to take steps toward a goal without recording them, thinking I'll remember. Before I know it, weeks have passed, and I haven't done what I planned.

Waiting Mode

Think of this as a void of time between now and the time you have plans. It feels impossible to start, continue or finish any tasks. So, you just wait anxiously. You can't do anything useful during that time. All you can do is worry about being late for the later appointment. This is a big one for me, as while I may never be late (apart from writing this chapter), when I have an important appointment or need to be somewhere at a certain time, I'm either in waiting mode or I turn up an hour or so early.

Starting Tasks, Procrastination and Task Paralysis

There can be many reasons why ADHDers struggle to start tasks or procrastinate. This is especially true when the task is so boring. Our interest-based nervous system isn't being sparked. Sometimes we don't know where to begin a task and as such we can't get started. Living in a world not made for us, ADHDers can have strong negative beliefs about ourselves and doubt our abilities. We tend to predict failure, even before starting. Added to this, many ADHDers struggle with perfectionism. We are constantly striving to prove that we are not a total fuck up. So we procrastinate, spend time doing other things to avoid the fear of failure. Or we are paralyzed, feeling like we are frozen and unable to do anything apart from ruminating about what we "should" be doing. The only thing to break this is usually the looming deadline, as that's when our fear-based nervous system kicks in.

Hyperfocus

The ADHD brain loves to hyperfocus on things, especially things the ADHDer enjoys. Once in a hyperfocus the ADHDer is "in the zone" and time becomes non-existent to them. We lose ourselves in what we are doing. This can be a wonderful place to be.

But, it can also lead to burnout, missed deadlines and poor performance at work or at home. It can affect our physical health, as when in hyperfocus, we can forget to eat, drink fluids and even go to the bathroom for hours on end. Also an important point for the non-ADHDer– we don't get to pick our hyperfocus. Yes, we would love to hyperfocus on getting our work done, eating well, getting fit, etc. but if it does not spark our interest-based nervous system, it is never going to happen!

Transitioning Between Tasks

Some ADHDers struggle to start tasks. Others struggle to stop them. I'm a bit of both, depending on what the task is. There can also be issues with switching tasks. It takes a lot of energy for an ADHDer to stop one thing and start another. This is especially true if it is unrelated to what we have been doing. This can lead people to feeling irritated, tired or overwhelmed.

Difficulty Managing Distractions

Remember that ADHD isn't a lack of attention. It's more like having too much attention and being unable to focus it. This can make ADHDers very distractible and as such, affect our ability to manage time. As an example, I'm a nightmare in a shared office–not only am

I distracted by everyone else, I am also very distracting to them too.

Celebrating Side Quests

I'm not a gamer, but I know there are side quests in computer games. They are extra challenges that you can do alongside the main quest. They don't affect the main game and may not even be related to the game at all! But, side quests can make it more fun for the player and enhance their playing experience.

What has this to do with ADHD, you might be wondering? And no, I haven't gone off on a tangent. Not this time anyway.

Think about this scenario, and it may be one you may know very well: You make a plan to do something, let's say it's to take the washing out of the machine and hang it up to dry. Off you go to the washing machine. As you make your way there, you notice another "little" thing that needs to be done. For example, a coat that could be hung up lying on the hallway stairs. So you go to hang up the coat, then once you have done that you spot some mail that needs to be read and put away. You gather that up and head to wherever it is you do that task. While on the way, you feel the need to go to the bathroom. Once there, you notice that you're nearly out of soap. So, head off to get more soap...and on and on, until you have forgotten what you started doing. It was taking the washing out. If you're anything like me you would have forgotten that by now.

(And while I have your attention–if you *do* have washing in the machine, now is your time to go and get it out and hang it up. Put the book down and do it now otherwise you'll forget. I'm just off to sort mine out...)

Now that we've sorted out the washing (and any other side quests along the way), let's get back to what I've been talking about.

Lots of ADHDers get frustrated by scenarios like the one I mentioned above. This only causes stress and anxiety. That, in turn, dysregulates us, making it even harder for us to get our tasks done.

What has helped me and others I know is to look at it another way. I reframe them so they are something good, not bad. In the scenario above, I would have put a coat away that has probably been on the stairs for weeks. The mail would have been sorted and I would not be out of soap next time I go to the loo. That's a lot of really helpful little things to tick off an imaginary to-do list.

On my journey to writing this chapter, my side quests involved making a pot of coffee, brushing and hoovering my hallway and living room and sorting some invoices. Yes, I didn't need to do them when I was planning to write. But, doing them, and more importantly, not beating myself up for doing them, has helped me feel much better overall.

Managing time effectively is crucial for anyone, but especially for ADHDers. Ignoring these challenges can lead to so many problems. Without proper time management, important tasks may be forgotten or left unfinished, leading to increased stress, missed deadlines and strained relationships. Procrastination and disorganisation can hinder personal and professional growth, limiting opportunities and success. However, when we work to combat these issues, the opposite can be said. With better time management comes reduced stress, increased self-confidence and a greater sense of accomplishment.

Combatting Time Management Issues

Work Backwards

When you need to be somewhere or have something done by a certain time, go to the end of the task. That is, go to the appointment or deadline time, then plan your time backwards. For example, if you have an appointment at 1pm, work out how long it takes to get to the location to figure out what time you have to leave your house. Then, think about how long it takes for you to get ready to leave. Work backwards as much as you need to until you have an action plan.

Use Alarms and Reminders

Alarms and reminders can help stop you from always checking the clock to be on time for appointments. This helps in allowing you to focus on other things in the time leading up to the appointment. You may need to set multiple ones and get into the habit of only dismissing them once you have taken action. You can also set them to distract you and bring you out of a hyperfocus, as I know some people who set alarms to remind them to eat or drink water throughout the day.

Apps That Help with Focus and Productivity

I have an app on my computer that takes all of my appointments from my online diary and puts them in one place. Every day, the app makes me start by planning. I use information from my diary and the tasks I need to get done that day. I also have to estimate how long the tasks will take. If it looks as if I am trying to put too much into my day, the app will give me a warning. There is even a function where I can time tasks. At the start of using this app, I thought it was going to take too much time (I hate daily planning) but in reality, it is quick and easy and has helped me see how long tasks really take, and not just how long I think about doing the task.

Noise-Cancelling Headphones

These can help to minimise distractions from noises around you when you are trying to concentrate. When I need to focus on important things, such as writing, I also listen to music designed to help neurodivergent brains stay focussed. Although, this sometimes works too well, as I've just realised I haven't eaten in hours and it is well past lunchtime. So make sure you set some alarms to remind you when to stop and eat!

Visual Timers

Visual timers can help ADHDers in many different ways. They can help us see how long we are spending on tasks or signal when it is time to move away from one task to another. Visual timers can also be a powerful motivator, helping you stay on task for the allotted time. For me, they also show how long I have to endure something I don't want to do before I can stop. They can also help us with time blindness. Over time, we learn how long tasks really take. Which helps us get better at estimating time.

Break Tasks Down Into Smaller Actions

Breaking tasks down helps to combat overwhelm and improve focus as we are just concentrating on one step in the process, not the whole task in of itself. Completing each action can also give us a hit of dopamine, which also helps with motivation. While I tend to ask a friend to help me with this when I'm struggling to break tasks down, lots of ADHDers are using AI platforms, such as ChatGPT or Goblin Tools to help them with this.

Beware of "ADHD Planners"

More and more, I see planners marketed as the ultimate solution for managing ADHD. People buy these planners with high hopes, start using them diligently, but quickly lose interest or misplace them. Then they move on to the next promising planner, wondering why none seem to work for them and feeling like something must be wrong with *them* and not the planners. Please, stop spending money on things that aren't working for you. There is no planner that can help everyone with or without ADHD. We each have to plan our time differently, and it may take a bit of trial and error. For one person, a physical book might be effective; for another, a whiteboard. Some might prefer an online diary. Personally, I use a combination of an online diary, phone reminders, a whiteboard and computer software.

Remember, time management with ADHD can sometimes feel like we are juggling flaming swords while riding a unicycle, blindfolded. And yes, even with the strategies above, you will still fuck up at times. It's not just you, we all do it. Successful time management is about finding strategies that work for you, and progress is made one step at a time. Celebrate your victories, learn from your setbacks and keep moving forward with confidence. When you inevitably stumble and mess up, just remember: Even the best time travellers occasionally miss their stop and end up in the wrong century. So, laugh it off, recalibrate and get back on track. Tomorrow is another day.

Chapter 5
Navigating the Storm

"Only when we are brave enough to explore the darkness
will we discover the infinite power of our light."
– Brené Brown

Has anyone ever told you that you are "too emotional" or that you overreact? Such as when a friend cancels plans at the last minute and you are left feeling sad for hours or maybe even days, wondering what you have done to offend them?

Does it sometimes feel like your moods swing from one extreme to the other? One minute, you're feeling happy and full of energy, then without any clear trigger, you're feeling pissed off at everything and your mood has crashed.

You're not alone. Many ADHDers struggle to regulate their emotions, leading to various negative outcomes.This can include difficulties in managing relationships, like overreacting to minor disagreements or feeling deeply hurt by perceived slights. At work, challenges can arise from intense emotional reactions to feedback or impulsive decision-making. Additionally, emotional dysregulation can cause trouble focusing on tasks, leading to missed deadlines and reduced productivity. Socially, it might result in withdrawing from friends or family due to fear of rejection or misinterpreting social cues, causing unnecessary conflicts.

All is not lost. Though we may struggle to regulate our emotions, by recognising how ADHD affects how we respond emotionally, we can develop strategies to manage our reactions more effectively. This, in turn, helps to improve our relationships as we become more aware of our triggers and learn to better communicate our needs to others. It can also enhance our work performance by helping us handle feedback and stress more constructively. Additionally, understanding emotional dysregulation can reduce feelings of isolation, as we realise that others share similar experiences.

Emotional Regulation

Emotional regulation, in its most basic terms, is our ability to manage our emotions. Being able to regulate our emotions is crucial because they affect how we think and act.

Unregulated emotions can wreak havoc in various ways. They can make you act impulsively, respond disproportionately to situations (like blowing up over minor issues), leave you feeling overwhelmed by a whirlwind of emotions and make it hard to pinpoint exactly what you're feeling. Reflecting on my own experiences, I realise that I've often been dysregulated, though I used to brush it off as me being a bit of a "drama queen". There are times when I feel overwhelmed by whatever is going on, but instead of acknowledging it, I become impatient and cranky, snapping at others or retreating into passive-aggressive silence.

Research shows that those with ADHD feel emotions more intensely than those without it, with 30-70% of adults with ADHD having difficulties regulating their emotions.

Why might this be the case?

Without getting too scientific, the part of our brain that controls our reaction to emotions is the amygdala, which is the part of the brain linked to the "fight or flight" responses when we feel we are in danger. When we feel an emotion–for example, worry or anxiety–a message is sent from the amygdala to the cerebral cortex. The cerebral cortex, in addition to dealing with emotions, also plays a key role in things such as memory, reasoning and problem solving. It allows the individual to take a breath and start to think things over.

However, within the ADHD brain, this connection is weak, meaning that we may not get the signal to take a breath, or the emotion is so strong that the signal is lost, and we react instead of thinking things over and working out a plan.

It's not hard to imagine that mood swings, intense emotional reactions and impulsive behaviours can have a detrimental impact on personal and professional relationships. Forming and maintaining relationships, something which is a basic human need and function, can be very difficult for someone experiencing emotional dysregulation.

As if this isn't bad enough, ADHDers are also at an increased risk of experiencing comorbid mental health conditions, such as depression and anxiety. This, in turn, can lead to the use of alcohol and drugs to self-medicate these conditions. Research shows that at some point in their lives, up to 50% of adults with ADHD have abused substances. This method of self-medicating can make emotional regulation even more difficult and have further negative impacts on work and personal lives.

Rejection Sensitive Dysphoria (RSD)

Rejection Sensitive Dysphoria, also known as RSD, is when someone feels extremely hurt or upset by even small signs of rejection or criticism. In the words of Laura Mears-Reynolds, from the *ADHDAF Podcast*, "RSD is just really shit daydreams, don't believe everything you think."

However, despite the "dysphoria" label, RSD is not an official diagnosis. Instead it is linked to emotional dysregulation. Rejection hits differently for ADHDers, as it's not just a "meh, that was a bummer" kind of thing. For us it can be like we have been punched in the gut.

Emotional dysregulation refers to difficulties in managing and controlling your emotions, whereas RSD specifically focuses on the intense emotional response to perceived rejection or criticism. ADHDers experience an exaggerated and overwhelming reaction to rejection, often feeling deeply hurt or devastated even by minor instances of criticism or disapproval. For example, you've sent a text to your mate, you can see they've read it but haven't replied. Some people may think their mate is busy and hasn't had time to reply, whereas, thanks to

RSD, you believe your mate is upset with you and doesn't want to be your friend anymore. That is why they have not responded.

Imagine RSD as having a set of super-sensitive emotional antennae that pick up on every hint of disapproval, real or imagined. Every hint of possible rejection triggers a painful reaction, both physical and emotional.

Depending on the individual, reactions can be either internal or external. When internalised, it can resemble a depressive episode and, for some, lead to suicidal ideation. This can come on so fast that it can also be misdiagnosed as rapid cycling bipolar disorder. Externalised RSD can present as a full-on tantrum or rage at the situation or person responsible for causing the pain.

Those who struggle with RSD tend to respond by becoming people pleasers, losing sight of their own ambitions and goals as they focus on making everyone around them happy, ensuring they like them and don't disapprove of them. Some become overachievers, constantly striving for perfection, while others just give up and stop trying to do things as it is so anxiety-provoking.

Spotting RSD in Yourself and Others

How RSD presents itself will differ from person to person, but below are some signs you may spot in yourself or others experiencing RSD.

Feeling like you are on an emotional rollercoaster.
One minute you're flying high, and the next, crashing into sadness or anger–all because of a perceived slight. RSD can make your emotions swing wildly in response to social cues.

Social withdrawal.
The fear of rejection may stop you from putting yourself out there. You might cancel plans last minute, avoid social gatherings or stay quiet in groups for fear of judgement. This withdrawal can be a way of protecting yourself from the anticipated rejection and pain.

Your inner critic is at maximum volume.
You are your harshest critic, constantly berating yourself for perceived mistakes or dwelling on past rejections and failures. Negative self-talk fuels feelings of worthlessness and makes it hard for you to see your own value.

Obsessively replaying past criticisms in your mind.
Analysing every detail and imagining the worst-case scenario for future interactions. Rumination can trap you in a cycle of anxiety and fear, making it difficult to move forward.

Relationship challenges.
Feeling constantly on guard in relationships, interpreting neutral comments as attacks and jumping to defensive conclusions. This tension can make it difficult to build trust and intimacy with others.

RSD nearly led to me giving up on writing this book before I'd even started. At the beginning of January 2024, after signing up with Chloë at Inspired By Publishing to get support with writing the book, I was telling a group of fellow ADHD coaches (and friends) about the book and my idea behind it. They were really enthusiastic, thinking it was a great idea and telling me they couldn't wait to read it. However, in true ADHD style, they started talking about their own ideas for ADHD books, and immediately I felt sick. My head started swimming with thoughts such as, "No-one will read my book... they could do it so much better than me... I'm delusional... I'm not good enough," and so on.

In the past, before I knew about ADHD in my life and learned about emotional regulation and RSD, I would have kept quiet about how I was feeling and what I was thinking. I might have given up on my dream of being an author and my goal of helping other perimenopausal, late-diagnosed ADHDers. Not this time. This time, I acknowledged what was going on, recognised it as RSD, and spoke to my friends about it in the moment instead of stewing on it. For me, recognising and calling RSD out for what it is has been one of the most effective tools I have to combat it.

Which leads me nicely to looking at ways we can learn to regulate our emotions and help with RSD.

Regulate Your Emotions and Manage RSD

Identify Your Strengths

Make a list of your strengths and what you like about yourself. This can be difficult to start with as we often struggle to see the positives in ourselves. If you need help with this, ask someone who knows you well what they think your strengths are and what they think you are good at. You can also search online for questionnaires that can help you identify your strengths.

Keep a "Smile File"

Save thank-you cards, emails and notes. Take pictures of things you have done well or been successful at. Gather motivational quotes. Write down things people say that make you feel good about yourself. Keep a note of the good things that happen to you. And when you are experiencing RSD or having doubts about yourself, read through all of these. While you can do this electronically, I think it is more impactful to have them in a physical file or scrapbook.

Use a Cognitive Reframing Technique

This is something you can do at any time and in any place to shift your mindset and look at a situation, person or relationship from a different angle. One way of doing this is to ask yourself the following questions:

- **What am I feeling right now?**
  (Disappointed, confused, furious.)

- **What happened to make me feel this way?**
  (They brushed my concerns off in the meeting with no explanation.)

- **Does the situation have a different explanation that might make sense?**
  (Maybe they're stressed, sick or dealing with something else they don't feel comfortable

explaining. They might plan to explain more when they can.)

- **What do I want to do about these feelings?** (Scream, vent my frustration by throwing things, text back something rude.)

- **Is there a better way of coping with them?** (Ask if everything's OK. Ask if you can have a conversation about it later in the week. Go for a walk or run.)

By considering possible alternatives, you're reframing your thoughts, which can help you modify your initial extreme reaction. It can take some time before this response becomes a habit. With practice, going through these steps in your head will become easier and more effective.

As ADHDers, learning to regulate our emotions and navigate RSD is about progress over perfection. There may never be a time when you or I will have fully mastered these challenges. We are human, after all.

However, every step you take towards understanding and managing your emotions is a victory in itself. If you have a setback, use it as a reminder to practise self compassion and see it as an opportunity to learn and strengthen your emotional resilience.

It does get easier, I can testify to that. Remember, you are capable, resilient and never alone on this journey.

Chapter 6
Burnout

"You will burn and you will burn out: You will be healed
and come back again."
– Fyodor Dostoyevsky

It might just be me, but I don't recall burnout being discussed much before the Covid-19 pandemic in 2020, do you? Nowadays, it seems to be a topic high on many workplace agendas. Perhaps it was being talked about before, but I missed it due to my time in the army, where we definitely weren't talking about it. However, in my particular part of the army there was a lot of sickness due to "stress", with the slight undercurrent that this was also a failure of the individual to "manage their stress". On reflection, it's no wonder we didn't talk about it.

So, what is burnout? The World Health Organisation (WHO) describes it as "a state of physical and emotional exhaustion" linked to unmanaged long term work stress. Personally, I describe it as "constantly feeling like shit!!'" For me, it feels as if one of Harry Potters' Dementors has come along and sucked every bit of happiness and energy out of every cell in my body and mind, turning me into one of them.

So, what is burnout? The World Health Organisation (WHO) describes it as "a state of physical and emotional exhaustion" linked to unmanaged long-term work stress". Personally, I describe it as "constantly feeling like shit!" For me, it feels as if one of Harry Potter's Dementors has come along and sucked every bit of happiness and energy out of every cell in my body and mind, turning me into one of them.

ADHD burnout is similar to the WHO description, but the cause is due to unmanaged ADHD symptoms rather than work-related stress specifically. With ADHD burnout, in addition to physical and mental exhaustion, there is an added emotional exhaustion aspect.

ADHDers are vulnerable to burnout, with research showing that we have a 50% higher risk of burnout compared to non-ADHDers, with up to 93% of us experiencing burnout symptoms, compared to 30% of the general population.

Throughout my life, not knowing I had ADHD, I hit many points where I was mentally and physically exhausted, which I now know was actually burnout. During those times, I would "pull myself together", or as I now know it, firmly attach my "mask" to hide my internal struggles, feeling too embarrassed and ashamed to let others know I was struggling. On the outside, I was a strong, capable soldier–while inside I felt like a complete failure.

Then, towards the end of 2021, I hit the lowest point I can remember. I was tearful all the time, my memory started to fail me and the fog engulfing my brain was seriously affecting my mental health. I had experienced depression before, but this was worse—so much so that I worried I was developing early onset dementia. Perimenopause had entered my life. The symptoms that I now know to be ADHD, which had always been in the background, became unmanageable. No matter how hard I tried, my mask would not stay on. I could not "pull myself together". This was the start of my longest period of burnout to date, which lasted until around the time I decided to write this book in October 2023.

Identifying ADHD Burnout

Burnout can sneak up on any of us, even those of us who seem to be managing on the surface. If you are wondering whether you or someone close to you might be experiencing it, take some time to reflect on how you're feeling in different aspects of your life. Use the guide questions below:

Emotional

- Do you feel like you're constantly running on empty?
- Are you emotionally drained and unable to recharge?
- Have you lost interest in things you used to find joy in?
- Are you easily frustrated, irritable or impatient, more than before?
- Do you feel numb?

Physical

- Are you constantly tired and lacking energy, even after getting enough sleep?
- Have your sleep patterns changed, making it difficult to fall asleep or stay asleep?
- Are you experiencing more frequent headaches, tension in your muscles or stomach problems?
- Have you noticed any changes in your appetite or weight?

Behavioural

- Do you feel less motivated to do things you used to enjoy?
- Are you procrastinating more than usual?
- How is your concentration, are you struggling to focus on even simple tasks?
- Have you stopped being social?
- Are you drinking more alcohol or caffeine as a way of coping?

Cognitive

- Have you become more forgetful or started having difficulties remembering details?
- Do you feel mentally foggy or struggling to make decisions that were easy before?
- Is it harder for you to process information or solve problems effectively?

Extra Consideration for ADHDers

For those with ADHD, burnout makes existing challenges harder. We need to check in on ourselves regularly. We should ask ourselves:

- Is it getting harder to manage executive function tasks? (This includes planning, organising and time management.

- Are your emotions more volatile, making it harder to regulate them?
- Are you hyperfocusing more frequently, but feeling even more drained and depleted afterwards?
- Are you using procrastination as a coping mechanism due to overwhelm and fear of failure?

It's important to remember that we all have different experiences of burnout. If you're worried you may be heading that way or are already there, speak to someone. This could be your GP, employer, therapist, a trusted friend or even an ADHD coach

Embracing Your Strengths to Combat Burnout

Identifying and embracing strengths can help ADHDers build resilience and thrive, helping us combat burnout. ADHDers can find it difficult to see their strengths, probably due to the amount of negative comments they have heard about themselves–or even thought about themselves–throughout their lives. It's estimated that by the age of 12, ADHDers will have heard over 20,000 negative things said about them by others, such as their parents, teachers and peers. If you then add that to all the years late-diagnosed ADHDers go without a diagnosis, how many more will they have heard? How many more will they have told themselves?

So how do you go about finding your strengths? Consider these questions:

- What activity do you do where you get into the flow of it, losing all sense of time?

- What are you naturally good at?

- What problems do you enjoy solving?

- What makes you feel happy, energised and engaged?

- If you could teach someone else a skill or share knowledge about something, what would it be?

- What do you find easy to do that others seem to struggle doing?

If you struggle to answer them for yourself, ask someone you trust to answer them for you.

Once you have identified your strengths, think about how much you use them in your life. This will be an ongoing process. Balance is really important—ADHDers can burn out through the underuse just as much as the overuse of our strengths. For example, hyperfocusing on something we enjoy to the exclusion of rest or the stress brought on by boredom.

Recovering From and Preventing Burnout

It is important to know that it can take time to recover from ADHD burnout. Some things that can help with recovery and prevent further episodes of burnout are:

- Prioritise sleep. Sleep is vital for the healing of body and mind. Burnout will have affected the quantity and quality of your sleep.
- Focus on rest and relaxation. Take time away from whatever caused the burnout. Find activities that promote rest and relaxation. This will look different for each of us. Some examples include meditation, mindfulness, breathwork, regular massages, Reiki or yoga.
- Regulate emotions. Learn how to regulate your emotions and engage in healthy coping mechanisms such as exercise or being creative. Practise mindfulness and relaxation techniques.
- Spend more time unmasked. Masking is stressful in itself and can lead to burnout. Spend time with people who accept you exactly as you

are. Seek out people and places where you can be your true self.

- Outsource executive functioning tasks. Identify the tasks that take up most of your energy (either from doing or avoiding doing). Then, identify how you can delegate them. You can then use this freed-up mental energy for the tasks you enjoy doing.

- Attend to your sensory needs. Start to notice how you feel. When you start to feel overwhelmed, take breaks. Work out what your senses need to reduce overwhelm. Consider using things such as fidget toys, adapted lighting, weighted blankets or noise-cancelling headphones

- Set boundaries. People with ADHD often have less energy to give others. Set boundaries with those in your life. Avoid overcommitting your time and energy. Prioritise self-care activities such as sleep, hobbies and spending time with loved ones. Learn to say no when needed.

- Engage in activities you enjoy. They help ease burnout by bringing you joy and restoring your energy.

- Manage your time. Avoid overwhelm by building routines, setting realistic goals, using tools like diaries and planners (online or digital, whatever suits you) and breaking down large tasks into manageable ones.

- Request for accommodations at work. Having the right support in place at work can help to prevent burnout. We'll look at this in more detail in Chapter 8.

Recovery is not always a straightforward process. You may have some setbacks along the way. The important thing is to be patient with yourself. Keep taking small steps. Focus on self-care. Get support if you need it.

Chapter 7
Navigating Relationships
With ADHD

"Patience is imperative if you love someone with ADHD."
– Katherine Quie

Relationships are a big part of our lives, and it will come as no surprise that ADHD can have a significant impact on them. Of all the topics I have written about in this book, undiagnosed ADHD has had the most impact on my relationships with others, whether they be friends, family or romantic partners.

Humans are social creatures, and we are involved in a number of different relationships, whether that be as a parent to a child, working with colleagues at work, friends, family or romantic partners. Relationships with others are already hard enough due to our individuality and different upbringings and social backgrounds. Plus, let's be honest here, how many of us have ever been taught how to have a relationship with another person? Not anyone I know, that's for sure. Our information on how to make and keep relationships comes from what we see around us while growing up: TV programmes, films, books, social media, etc.

Yes, I know there are some people who are perfectly happy with minimal interaction with others. Good for them, but that's not me, nor do I imagine it is you either if you are reading this chapter. Healthy relationships can add so much to our lives–they give us connection, a sense of belonging and there's tons of research out there that tells us there is a positive impact on our mental and physical health. People in happy relationships live longer, whereas the opposite is true for those who feel lonely and isolated.

I've spent most of my life believing that I was a bad partner. A serial monogamist. I have moved from one failed relationship to the next with hardly a gap between. In December 2022, shortly after receiving my ADHD diagnosis and while still unaware of the complete impact of undiagnosed ADHD on my life, history repeated itself. After about 18 months together, my partner ended our relationship. Leaving me battered and bruised once again by love.

This left me confused, wondering where I had gone wrong this time. Why had I not been enough for her. Added to the usual self-recrimination for yet another failed relationship, I realised I could not enter another relationship until I understood more about myself and the impact undiagnosed ADHD may have had on my relationships. So off I went, further down the rabbit hole of research.

Challenges ADHDers May Face in Relationships

There are a number of things that make it difficult for ADHDers to create and maintain healthy relationships. Here are a few to be aware of:

Hyperfocus Dating

At the beginning of a relationship, ADHDers can hyperfocus on the other person, making them feel as if they are the centre of their world, showering them with attention, gifts and time. However, when the hyperfocus stops (as all hyperfocus does), the change can be dramatic. The non-ADHDer may wonder what changed, thinking we no longer want to be with them. This can be confusing for the ADHDer if they are not aware that this is a problem. Our ADHD brains always seek novelty, which can lead some ADHDers to look elsewhere once it has worn off in their current relationship.

I also want to make it *very* clear that hyperfocus dating is different from "love bombing". Love bombing is a conscious act by a person to influence the other through extreme affection. Hyperfocus dating is often about novelty and is done unintentionally or subconsciously, whereas love bombing is about manipulation and is a calculated action.

Communication Difficulties

ADHDers can often lack social interaction skills. It can be hard for us to not talk nonstop. We drift in and out of conversations or focus them just on ourselves. We can go off on tangents or forget what is being discussed– even mid-conversation! For me, I'm a verbal processor which means for me to process information correctly, I have to talk it out loud. This hasn't been helpful for disagreements. Some of what I say isn't what I actually want to say in response. But, to get to my point, I have to talk it out and "go around the houses" at times.

As we know, ADHDers can be very easily distracted, leading us to pay little attention to our partners or fail to follow through on promises, especially when undiagnosed. Partners may see this as uncaring or rude, potentially causing a lot of hurt and disagreements.

Emotional Dysregulation

ADHDers generally tend to feel emotions strongly and wear their hearts on their sleeves. Any form of rejection is painful, and coupled with Rejection Sensitive Dysphoria (RSD), it can feel unbearable. As ADHDers move further into a relationship, we may start to let our guard down. The highs, lows and our sensitivity may become more obvious to the other person, leading to communication issues, mood swings and emotional outbursts. This, in turn, can leave partners feeling on edge or like they are walking on eggshells.

Forgetfulness

This can impact many aspects of a relationship, such as forgetting to pay bills or missing important dates like birthdays and anniversaries. I'm guilty of the latter; an ex-partner once handed me a card just after we'd woken up one morning. I remember thinking, "Oh, that's nice. I wonder what it is," only to open it and see it was an anniversary card. With a confused look on my face, I said, "But our anniversary isn't until Thursday," to which my very hurt girlfriend replied, "It is Thursday!" I can still remember wishing the ground would swallow me up. I was never forgiven for that mistake, thinking I'd just forgotten because I was busy at work. I never considered looking back to see that I'm also very bad at remembering birthdays.

I've also been guilty of forgetting household chores. If I have a to-do list and a timeframe, they get done–but at the last minute, when I know my partner is due home anytime. When I've explained this to ex-partners before, they've said things like, "I'm not your mother. I should not have to write you a list," or "I've enough to do without also having to write you a list." My response at the time was, "Fine, well, they just won't get done then, will they." You can imagine what happened next.

Impulsivity

This is a common problem, leading to overspending on things you really don't need. BOGOF (Buy One Get One Free) offers used to be a minefield for me. I never needed one of the items on offer, let alone two or more. But, at that time, offering me something that looked like a great deal, and it was hard not to put it into my cart. That was okay when it was my money, but it has led to many arguments in the past when it is "our" money. Thankfully, I am much better with this now. Impulsivity in relationships can also manifest as blurting out inappropriate comments, which in the past I've done far too many times to remember. I also think I'm whispering these comments, which apparently, I'm not. For some ADHDers, it can also show up by getting into inappropriate relationships or having risky sex.

Intimacy and Sex

Sex is still a fairly taboo topic, so it's not surprising that the impact of ADHD symptoms on sex is not talked about much either. ADHD symptoms can affect our ability to be intimate with partners in various ways, depending on how they affect us individually. For example, thanks to executive functioning difficulties, for some ADHDers initiating sex can feel like too much effort, leading to low sex drive. Emotional dysregulation is linked to high and low sex drives. Sensory processing can make ADHDers become under-stimulated or overstimulated. Understimulation generally happens once the excitement and novelty have worn off, while overstimulation could be either good or bad. Heightened senses can make sex more enjoyable, but if sensations like touch or sound become too intense, sex can become unpleasant. ADHDers may also hyperfocus on sex.

At times, I've struggled with being distracted during sex. It wasn't until I started listening to the podcast "ADHD as Females" that I realised it was linked to

ADHD. More importantly, I was not a weirdo. There are many other women like me–phew! I remember feeling so confused when in the middle of an intimate moment with a partner. Despite enjoying what was happening. A random thought such as, "Have you spoken to…? Or did you remember to…?" would come into my head. Thankfully, I never said these things. But can you imagine the battle of trying to "stay on task" while having these random thoughts in your head? Or can you imagine, blurting out to your partner in the middle of sex, "Did you get to speak to your aunt?" Maybe if you're reading this book, you can.

Strengthening Relationships as an ADHDer

We have already covered ways to tackle time management, memory problems and emotional dysregulation. If they are impacting your relationships, head back to the relevant chapters.

Self-Awareness is Key

For me, knowing ourselves is the most important starting point for relating to others. Self-awareness is not just about being aware of how we behave, think and feel. It's about working out why and deciding what we will do differently if needed, all through the lens of

ADHD and how it affects us individually. Yes, ADHD can cause us to forget dates and have trouble with emotions, but it's no excuse for ongoing bad behaviour or not trying to cope with our struggles.

For example, now that I know about hyperfocus dating and that it's not just me picking the wrong woman to date, I will be ready for it when I dip my toe back into the dating pool. I know I will have to regulate my hyperfocus and, when the time comes, find ways to tackle the lack of novelty. This is, of course, if she is truly the right woman for me and I'm not acting impulsively out of loneliness.

You could start by asking yourself these questions:

- What do I struggle with in relationships?
- What do I find easy in relationships?
- How has my ADHD affected me in past relationships?
- How does my ADHD affect my current relationship (if you are in one)?
- What can I do that helps me with these struggles?
- Who do I know that can help me?

Communicate, Communicate, Communicate

The better we are at communicating, the better our relationships. Good communication in relationships inevitably leads to more trust. It also leads to better conflict resolution, more intimacy and increased happiness. However, communication isn't just a one way thing, both partners need to feel heard and understood. Yes, this can be hard for ADHDers, as we talk incessantly when given half a chance. But, this doesn't come easily to those without ADHD either. We should not have to mask in our relationships. As such, we need to tell our partners about our ADHD and how it affects us. How else will they even begin to understand when we are having a meltdown over something that outwardly may seem trivial?

Manage Conflict

Some helpful strategies start first and foremost with emotional regulation. When emotions run high and we're not regulated, our ability to think clearly diminishes, often leading to unintended and hurtful remarks. Additionally, it's essential to recognise that we're not mind readers; assuming we know what our partner is thinking, especially when it leans towards negativity, can exacerbate conflicts.

When addressing issues with our partner, it's vital to stay focused on the present moment rather than dredging up past grievances repeatedly. Using "I" statements instead of "you" statements when expressing feelings can improve communication and prevent defensiveness. Sharing individual coping strategies for managing conflict within the relationship can help you understand each other better, as well. For example, when things get too overwhelming for me, I need a timeout. If I don't tell the other person this, me walking off in the middle of an argument can make things worse.

Ultimately, if you and your partner are not great at communicating, it may be a good idea to get some couples counselling to help. Remember, none of us have been taught this stuff, so this is in no way a failure.

Use Shared Strategies

These include things like shared calendars, shared reminders and shared to-do lists. These let both partners know what is happening or what to expect. Set these up together so that it doesn't feel as if one person is taking control or having to do all the work. As an example, a friend of mine and her partner made a list of all the household chores. They sat together and divided them based on their preferences. In truth, they chose the ones they hated the least (they both hate doing chores). She then set up an app that reminds them of the chores, which gives them a hit of dopamine when they get to tick the chore off the list.

You could also try body doubling, or even turning things into a game. I know someone who has gamified household chores for her whole family, both adults and kids. A day and time is scheduled, each person has their list, and it's a competition to see who gets theirs done (properly) first.

I know that it can feel like navigating relationships with ADHD is really hard. Here's the thing: While it's undeniably tough at times, understanding ourselves better and putting the strategies mentioned here into action can truly work wonders. Picture this: healthier, happier connections not just with romantic partners, but with everyone you meet. And guess what? I've seen it firsthand. I've got this incredible circle of friends, all thriving in their relationships despite navigating their own ADHD roller coasters. Plus, by using what I've learned while down this ADHD rabbit hole, it has changed how I relate to friends, family and even coworkers. So, if you're feeling a bit lost, just know that there's a path forward. One that leads to stronger, more fulfilling connections than you ever thought possible.

Chapter 8
Managing ADHD at Work

"Everybody is a genius. But if you judge a fish by its ability to climb a tree, it will live its whole life believing that it is stupid."

– Albert Einstein

Understanding ADHD is crucial for creating supportive environments. Historically, much attention has been given to how ADHD affects children and young people in education. But what happens once these children grow into adults? Or for those diagnosed later in life? What about the impact on work or further education? ADHD in adults has only been recognised in the UK since 2008, and although it has been 26 years since then, there is still a lot of scepticism. Maybe, like me, you were one of those sceptics? Or maybe you have people around you who "don't believe in ADHD"?

Navigating work as a late-diagnosed ADHDer can be confusing. Along the way, you will have already come up against problems where you have found workarounds or learnt to avoid tasks that are particularly difficult or draining. Maybe you've gone from job to job, either getting bored and looking for something more exciting, or getting fired for being "incompetent" (which, by the way, you were not). Maybe you impulsively quit when imposter syndrome or RSD took hold, fearing you'd be seen as incompetent (which, again, you are not).

Think back. Have you always found certain tasks challenging, yet believed they were normal for you, even though others seem to do them effortlessly? Have you had to secretly work twice or three times harder to get things done so that no-one thinks you are stupid or incompetent? Are there jobs that you wanted to apply for but felt you were not even in the running for an interview? Or is there a qualification you would like to get but the thought of having to sit still in a classroom turns you cold?

With the right support in place, ADHDers can have successful and fulfilling careers. Finding a role that aligns with your strengths can be key to this. For example, if you are someone who has a lot of energy and creativity, a career in marketing may play to your strengths. For me, my strengths lie in my love of learning and helping others, which has led me into coaching and training.

ADHD does not stop you from studying at university. For most of my life, I didn't think I was clever enough to get a degree; however, at the age of 43, I graduated with First Class Honours. The founders of ADHD Adults UK both have PhDs. Many successful entrepreneurs have a diagnosis of ADHD, often without any formal qualifications. Such as Richard Branson, the founder of the Virgin Group and Ingvar Kamprad, the founder of Ikea. It is even thought that Einstein would have qualified for a diagnosis of ADHD, dyslexia and autism.

What if you knew that you could get support in the workplace or education setting that would help you to have the career you wanted, including self-employment? Or support that would enable you to go back and study for that qualification you've dreamt of?

<u>Reasonable Workplace Adjustments</u>

At the time of writing this book, you're not obligated to tell your employer or potential employer about your ADHD diagnosis. However, if you do, they're legally required to provide support and accommodations for you.

Reasonable adjustments are changes made by employers to support ADHDers to carry out their role more effectively. This can be anything from flexible working hours, to special equipment or even just tweaking the environment to make it more accessible for the individual. These can make a huge difference because they level the playing field, allowing everyone to bring their A-game to work, no matter what challenges they might be dealing with. Plus, they make the workplace more welcoming and inclusive for everyone. It's a win-win, really.

You can ask for reasonable adjustments right from the beginning of a job application process. For example, if, like me, you struggle with "being put on the spot" during interviews because you don't know what questions you will be asked, you can ask to see the questions beforehand so it gives you time to prepare. For one job I applied for, they gave me the questions a week in advance; for another, it was the day before. This really helps me feel like I am bringing my best self to the interview, rather than "waffling" an answer that, in that moment, feels very incoherent. I have friends who have been given additional rest breaks during longer interview processes or had permission to take notes during an interview.

If you are already employed, you can ask for reasonable adjustments by speaking to your manager or employer. They will want to know what you feel you are struggling with and what will help. They may also request occupational health reports or something from your GP. Each workplace will differ.

While you do not need to tell your employer about your diagnosis of ADHD, you may not be able to do certain jobs while taking stimulant medication. For instance, you cannot train to be a pilot if you're on ADHD medication. To apply for reasonable adjustments, you need to disclose your diagnosis. Otherwise, you are not covered by employment law (UK only, I can't speak for other countries).

Employers in the UK must make reasonable workplace adjustments under the Equality Act 2010. This applies to employees or applicants with long-term disabilities, ensuring that they are not placed at a disadvantage compared to those without a disability. Examples of these adjustments can be:

- Adjustments to the work environment, such as a quiet space to work from when overwhelmed by open-plan offices. Some people I know have received standing desks, which help with discomfort from sitting for long periods. I have a standing desk at home, and it has been a game-changer for me. When I start fidgeting in my chair, I set it to rise, allowing me to move around while working.

- Changes to work patterns, this can include flexible working patterns or locations. This could involve a change to your starting/finishing times or the ability to manage your diary based on your energy/concentration levels. You may have the option of working solely from home, rather than going into a busy office, or a hybrid model where you spend some of your time at home and the rest in the office.

- Additional support, such as extra training, mentoring or coaching. This can be paid for by your employer, and there is UK government funding for this. This can include workplace coaching, which helps you build strategies to overcome your individual barriers at work. It can also include ADHD awareness training for your managers and team members so that they can learn about the impact of ADHD and how they can support those with a diagnosis. Additional support could also include regular meetings with your line manager, and not as a way of micromanaging you, but as a way of ensuring that you are getting what you need to do your best work.

Adjustments must be reasonable based on the employer's size, resources, type of work and impact on the business. They don't need to make changes that would affect the business's operations or result in high costs. If reasonable adjustments are not made, an employee can claim discrimination under the Equality Act.

An important note: More information on reasonable workplace adjustments is freely available online. ACAS is a good place to start for workplace advice and guidance. If you have a specific issue, seek help there.

Sounds great doesn't it? However, many people are afraid to ask for work adjustments due to stigma and lack of education in workplaces. I was one of them. As ADHDers who have lived a lot of our lives undiagnosed, we may be worried about the impact of telling our employers that we have ADHD or asking for adjustments. I worried that admitting to struggling at work might make others see me as incompetent. I feared being judged and losing professional standing at the university I was working in. After all, how can a mental health nurse support students with ADHD if she also needs adjustments? I also felt like a bit of a failure as I've been able to "manage" for the majority of my working life, up to this point. Looking back now and knowing what I now know, it seems silly to me to have thought that way. However, it was a real fear for me and after speaking to many other late diagnosed ADHDers, I know I was not alone. They had similar fears about "coming out" at work and seeking help.

For all the reasons above I was really nervous when I told my line manager about my diagnosis of ADHD in December 2022. While I did not want to disclose my diagnosis, I felt that I had no other option because I was really struggling at work. I was putting a lot of energy into hiding my struggles and it had already led to a period of time off work due to burn out. When I told her, she was very supportive and made a referral to occupational health. However, then came the most difficult question for me, "What is it that you are struggling with and what can we do to help?" I found this question really tricky. After working for over two decades and finding ways of getting things done, I was unsure about what support or adjustments could or would ease my life. ADHD coaching really helped me with this as it allowed me realise how I have been masking throughout my working life and what "hacks" I'd already come up with.

My team manager has also shown more interest in ADHD after I have shared my experiences. She has spent time learning more about it, giving us a shared language for discussing my struggles. It's also made me more confident to be myself and unmask as much as possible. Overall, this has made me feel happier at the university when at the beginning of 2022, I was ready to quit.

The sad thing is, I know I am one of the lucky ones.

Maybe you don't feel like you can disclose your ADHD to your employer. So what can you do? One of my friends does not want to tell her employer about her ADHD. However, she still needed something to change as, being in an open office, with all the chatter and distractions, was impacting her ability to concentrate and do her work. She overcame this by asking her manager if she could work from home more and when she was in the office, could she sit in a quieter spot. She also asked if it was okay to wear noise cancelling headphones when she was really struggling in the office. All of this was agreed and her employer still doesn't know she has ADHD.

For those I work with who are going for interviews and struggle with them, I encourage them to ask for reasonable adjustments to their interview. One recent coachee of mine, Anne (not her real name) was off work due to burnout from undiagnosed ADHD. She did not want to go back to her current workplace because it was so toxic and she knew she would be heading straight back into burnout in the not-so-distant future. She was applying for new jobs and getting through to the interview but progressing no further. Anne was clearly qualified for the roles she was applying for, so what was going wrong for her? When it came to the interview itself, she became completely overwhelmed when faced with questions she did not have time to prepare for. This led her to verbally process the answers, all in front of the interviewer/panel. As such, Anne worried that she had spoken or disclosed too much, and RSD was a big barrier to her being able to communicate effectively.

Anne had never asked for reasonable adjustments, being scared that her potential employer would prejudge her before meeting her. She also knew that having the interview questions beforehand would give her time to verbally process the question, helping her formulate her answer before even stepping into the interview. This would leave her free from the stress and anxiety of being put on the spot when asked questions she had not had time to prepare her answer for.

During one of our sessions, I asked her if she would want to work for an employer who might discriminate due to ADHD or reject her interview accommodation request. She said she would not and the next interview she secured, she took the brave step of asking for adjustments. They did not hesitate to say yes and even suggested additional changes to the interview. After the interview, she was very happy with how it went. Although she didn't get the job, she got to present her best self.

Access to Work Scheme (ATW)

In 2023, I applied for Access to Work (ATW), a UK Government scheme that supports those with disabilities or a mental or physical health condition to get or stay in work. This includes those who are self-employed. ATW can provide a grant to help pay for practical support, such as an ADHD workplace strategy coach or specialist equipment. The grant can also be used for help in managing mental health, such as 1:1 sessions with a therapist or mental health professional. Payment for communication support is also provided, like sign language interpreters. These grants do not need to be paid back, they are not based on income and they do not affect other benefits you may be entitled to.

For an up to date eligibility criteria and details of how to apply, please go to the government website. You can apply online through the website link or by calling the provided numbers.

Reasonable Adjustments in Adult Education

While this chapter has been about the workplace, I want to acknowledge that there are lots of late diagnosed ADHDers going back into education. Either due to their own interests or maybe as part of their continual professional development at work. As in the workplace, there is a lot of support available in schools and universities. Each adult education institution will have its own procedures for accessing reasonable adjustments so my advice is to contact them directly. The ones I have studied with have not needed a formal diagnosis of ADHD. A working diagnosis is enough to get the support. A working diagnosis basically means that you are not formally diagnosed but it is believed you need further assessment/investigation. Being on the ADHD assessment waiting list can be enough to prove a working diagnosis.

Conclusion

"All endings are beginnings.
We just don't know it at the time."
– Mitch Albom

As you reach the end of this book, I want to take a moment to celebrate you. Yes, *you*!

It's time to reflect on the incredible journey you've been on so far. From the moment you first suspected that there was something more to your quirks and struggles to the day you finally received your diagnosis.

It's probably been a rollercoaster ride of emotions. The relief of finally understanding why you felt different, the frustration of missed opportunities and misunderstood intentions, the moments of self-doubt and the questions of whether you'd ever find your place in the world. But through it all, you've persevered, showing incredible resilience, courage and strength.

Think back to all the times you thought you were alone in your struggles, only to now discover that there is a world full of women just like you. Each of us are navigating a similar path, facing similar challenges and yet finding our own unique ways to thrive.

But this is not the end. In fact, it's just the beginning. Armed with knowledge about your brain and how it works, you now have the power to rewrite your story. No longer constrained by society's expectations or your own self-imposed limitations, you are free to embrace your true self and live life on your own terms.

Sure, there will still be challenges along the way. ADHD doesn't magically disappear just because you have a diagnosis. But now, you have the tools and support you need to face those challenges head-on. Whether it's from developing strategies to manage your time and stay organised, from seeking therapy to address underlying issues like anxiety or low self-esteem or from simply giving yourself permission to take breaks and practice self-care, you are now better equipped to navigate the ups and downs of life with ADHD.

Remember, ADHD is not a curse—it's a part of who you are. Your hyperfocus enables you to delve deeply into subjects that fascinate you, your creativity is boundless, and your knack for thinking differently often results in innovative solutions. Embrace your uniqueness and honour the strengths that come with having a brain wired in its own special way.

As you move forward, remember to be kind to yourself, forgive yourself for past mistakes and celebrate your victories, no matter how small they may seem. Surround yourself with people who lift you up and believe in your potential, and don't be afraid to ask for help when you need it.

Above all, never forget that you are enough, just as you are. You don't need to change who you are to fit into society's mould or live up to someone else's expectations. Your worth is not defined by your accomplishments or productivity levels. It's inherent simply because you exist.

Reflect on the progress you've made since your diagnosis. Maybe you've started to understand your thought patterns and behaviours better. Perhaps you've developed new coping strategies that make your daily life a bit easier. Every step forward, no matter how small, is a testament to your strength and determination.

Take pride in your journey. Each struggle has shaped you into the resilient person you are today. Each triumph, no matter how modest it may seem, is a victory worth celebrating. Your journey is uniquely yours, and it's something to be proud of

Your ADHD is a part of your story, but it doesn't define your entire narrative. It's a chapter, not the whole book. You have the power to write the next chapters of your life with intention and purpose. The insights you've gained about yourself can guide you as you move forward, helping you create a life that aligns with your true self.

Seek out communities of like-minded individuals. Connect with other women who have ADHD, share your experiences and learn from theirs. There's a powerful sense of validation and understanding that comes from being part of a community that truly gets you. Together, you can uplift and support each other through the highs and the lows.

Invest in your well-being. Prioritise self-care, not just as an occasional treat, but as a fundamental part of your routine. Whether it's mindfulness practices, physical activity, creative outlets or simply taking time to rest, find what nourishes your mind and body. Your well-being is the foundation upon which you can build a fulfilling life.

Don't be afraid to dream big. ADHD doesn't limit your potential; it enhances it. Your unique way of thinking, your passion and your drive can lead you to incredible places. Set goals that excite you and take steps towards achieving them. Break them down into manageable tasks, celebrate your progress and keep moving forward.

Whenever you find yourself doubting your worth or wondering if you belong, just remember these words:

You are not broken.
You are not a burden.
You are a warrior.
And you are not alone.

Oh, and if people don't like you due to you having ADHD, then they can fuck off!!

Here's to the next chapter of your amazing adventure. May it be filled with love, laughter and countless moments of joy.

Much love,
Lou
Your fellow ADHDer

Additional Support

If you ever feel that you need additional support or guidance on your journey, please do not hesitate to reach out to me. I offer 1:1 and group coaching programmes to support ADHDers navigate the challenges and celebrate the victories that come with ADHD. You'll find me at <u>lou@louoconnell.co.uk</u>

References

ADDA Editorial Team, 'ADHD and Memory Challenges: The Top Science-Backed Ways to Boost Your Memory', *Attention Deficit Disorder Association*, 2023, https://add.org/adhd-memory-loss/, (accessed 09 May 2024).

ADHD UK. 'Adult ADHD Self Screening Tool', *ADHD UK*, 2024, https://adhduk.co.uk/adult-adhd-screening-survey/, (accessed 09 March 2024).

ADHD UK. 'History: ADHD Over the Years', *ADHD UK*, 2023, https://adhduk.co.uk/the-history-of-adhd/, (accessed 04 February 2024).

Additude Editors. "From Love Bombing to Boredom: Is ADHD to Blame for Mercurial Relationship Cycles?', *ADDitude*, 2023, https://www.additudemag.com/love-bombing-adhd-hyperfocus/, (accessed 18 April 2024).

Anker, E., Haavik, J. and Heir, T., 'Alcohol and Drug Use Disorders in Adult Attention-Deficit/Hyperactivity Disorder: Prevalence and Associations With Attention-Deficit/Hyperactivity Disorder Symptom Severity and Emotional Dysregulation', *World Journal of Psychiatry*, vol. 10, no. 9, 2020, pp. 202-211, doi:10.5498/wjp.v10.i9.202.

Astenvald, R. et al. 'Emotion Dysregulation in ADHD and Other Neurodevelopmental Conditions: A Co-Twin Control Study', *Child and Adolescent Psychiatry and Mental Health*, vol. 16, no. 1, 2022, doi:10.1186/s13034-022-00528-0.

Attoe, D.E. and Climie, E.A., 'Miss. Diagnosis: A Systematic Review of ADHD in Adult Women', *Journal of Attention Disorders*, vol. 27, no. 7, 2023, pp. 645-657, doi:10.1177/10870547231161533.

Broadway, C., 'High and low estrogen exacerbate ADHD symptoms in females: New theory', *ADDitude*, 2024, https://www.additudemag.com/low-estrogen-adhd-hormones-theory/ (accessed 05 May 2024).

Caldwell, M., 'Hormones and ADHD: The Missing Key', *ADDept.*, 2023, https://www.addept.org/living-with-adult-add-adhd/homones-and-adhd, (accessed 25 April 2024).

Centers for Disease Control and Prevention. "About Attention-Deficit / Hyperactivity Disorder (ADHD)", *CDC*, 2024, https://www.cdc.gov/adhd/about/?CDC_AAref_Val=https%3A%2F%2Fwww.cdc.gov%2Fncbddd%2Fadhd%2Ffacts.html, (accessed 24 April 2024).

Children and Adults With Attention-Deficit/Hyperactivity Disorder (CHADD), 'Bias About ADHD Leaves Many Women With a Late Diagnosis', *CHADD*, 2022, https://chadd.org/adhd-weekly/bias-about-adhd-leaves-many-women-with-a-late-diagnosis/, (accessed 09 February 2024).

Davis, C., et al. 'Attention-deficit/hyperactivity Disorder in Relation to Addictive Behaviors: A Moderated-Mediation Analysis of Personality-Risk Factors and Sex. *Frontiers in Psychiatry*, vol. 6, no. 47, 2015. https://doi.org/10.3389/fpsyt.2015.00047 (accessed 05 August 2024).

Dr. Hallowell: The ADHD Hallowell Centers, 'ADHD and Time', *Dr. Edward Hallowell and the Hallowell Centers*, 2023, https://drhallowell.com/2018/03/02/adhd-and-time-2/, (accessed 09 March 2024).

Langmaid, S. "ADHD and Memory Loss: What to Know", *WEBMD*, 2022, https://www.webmd.com/add-adhd/adult-adhd-memory-loss, (accessed 12 March 2024).

Elkin, R. 'Women and ADHD: How Menopause Can Affect Women With ADHD', *Psychiatry-UK*, 2023, https://psychiatry-uk.com/women-and-adhd-how-menopause-can-affect-women-with-adhd/, (accessed 25 March 2024).

Equality Act 2010 c15.

Giuditta, A. '8 ADHD Symptoms That Affect Your Sex Drive', 2022, https://www.getinflow.io/post/sex-drive-libido-adhd, (accessed 09 February 2024).

Hallowell, E. 'The Dangers of Undiagnosed Adult ADHD', *ADDitude*, 2024, https://www.additudemag.com/undiagnosed-adult-adhd-diagnosis-symptoms/, (accessed 18 April 2024).

Koseva, N., 'How Can ADHD Affect My Relationships?', *The ADHD Centre*, 2022, https://www.adhdcentre.co.uk/how-can-adhd-affect-my-relationships/, (accessed 26 February 2024).

Russell, J. et al., 'Number of ADHD Patients Rising, Especially Among Women', *Epic Research*, 2023, https://www.epicresearch.org/articles/number-of-adhd-patients-rising-especially-among-women, (accessed 14 April 2024).

Sosnoki, K. 'ADHD and Time Perception: Overcoming Lateness', *Psych Central*, 2022, https://psychcentral.com/adhd/cutting-down-on-chronic-lateness-for-adults-with-adhd, (accessed 09 February 2024).

Mandriota, M. 'ADHD in Women Vs. Men: Does Gender Play a Role in Symptoms?', *Psych Central*, 2022, https://psychcentral.com/adhd/adhd-and-gender, (accessed 17 April 2024).

McCarthy, L.F. 'Women, Hormones, and ADHD', *ADDitude*, 2023, https://www.additudemag.com/women-hormones-and-adhd/, (accessed 09 April 2024).

Orlov, M. '11 Rules for Fighting Right and Forgiving Faster', *ADDitude*, 2021, https://www.additudemag.com/marriage-communication-adhd-spouses/, (accessed 26 March 2024).

Orlov, M. '9 Ways ADHD May Strain Relationships', *ADDitude*, 2024, https://www.additudemag.com/adhd-divorce-rate-marriage-help/, (accessed 28 May 2024).

Reed Roberts, M. 'Menopause and ADHD', *Balance by Newson Health*, 2022, https://www.balance-menopause.com/menopause-library/menopause-and-adhd/, (accessed 14 May 2024).

Shaw P. et al., 'Emotion Dysregulation in Attention Deficit Hyperactivity Disorder', *American Journal of Psychiatry*, vol. 171, no. 3, 2014, pp. 276-293.

Suitor, K., 'The True Value of ADHD Side Quests, Rabbit Holes, and Tangents', *ADDitude*, 2024, https://www.additudemag.com/how-to-engage-students-adhd-interests/, (accessed 23 May 2024).

The Brain Charity, 'Why Neurodivergent Women Are Diagnosed With ADHD and Autism Later in Life, and What This Means for Their Careers', *The Brain Charity*, 2023, https://www.thebraincharity.org.uk/neurodivergent-women-adhd-autism-adults/, (accessed 19 March 2024).

Treas, S. 'ADHD burnout: Understanding the link between ADHD and Burnout', *GoodTherapy.org Therapy Blog* [web blog], https://www.goodtherapy.org/blog/adhd-burnout/#:~:text=According%20to%20research%2C%20up%20to,population%20(AID%2C%202019) (accessed 23 February 2024).

Wheeler, R.B. 'How ADHD Affects Your Relationship', *WebMD*, 2022, https://www.webmd.com/add-adhd/ss/slideshow-adhd-relationship-tips, (accessed 17 March 2024).

World Health Organization, 'Burnout an 'Occupational Phenomenon': International Classification of Diseases', *World Health Organization*, 28 May 2019, https://www.who.int/news/item/28-05-2019-burn-out-an-occupational-phenomenon-international-classification-of-diseases (accessed 23 January 2024).

www.ingramcontent.com/pod-product-compliance
Lightning Source LLC
Chambersburg PA
CBHW071232020426
42333CB00015B/1433